CHILDREN AND THE HOLY SPIRIT

To Steve, Paul and Vicki:
with love, thanks and our prayers that you'll always
follow God as passionately as you do now.

Children and the Holy Spirit

Leading Children into the Gifts and Fruit of the Spirit

Chris Leach

EASTBOURNE

First published in 1994 by Monarch Publications
as *And for Your Children*.
This completely updated and revised edition
published by Kingsway 2001.

Unless otherwise indicated, biblical quotations are
from the New International Version © 1973, 1978, 1984
by the International Bible Society.

ISBN 0 85476 917 X

Published by
KINGSWAY PUBLICATIONS
Lottbridge Drove, Eastbourne, BN23 6NT, England.
Email: books@kingsway.co.uk

Designed and produced for the publishers by
Bookprint Creative Services, P.O. Box 827, BN21 3YJ, England.
Printed in Great Britain.

Contents

Introduction

God spoke to me in a dream. The background was that the church where my husband was on the staff were looking for someone to become involved in the leadership of the children's ministry – a substantial task, since there were nearly 120 children up to the age of eleven. Because of my past involvement with children's ministry, I thought and prayed about it and talked to some trusted friends, but nothing within me felt called to respond. I did nothing, and felt perfectly at peace about it. But then, three months later, the dream came. I know dreams are only supposed to last for a few seconds, but I dreamt that I spent all the night debating with myself whether or not I should head up this ministry; a strange thing, since we had all felt so clearly that it was right for me not to become involved.

The next Sunday the service began, as it often did, with a plea for some parents to leave the church and go to help with the children, since their groups were so under-staffed. Immediately I *knew* I should go. I made my way over to the hall, and the sight that greeted me can only be described as complete chaos. Children were swinging around the pillars and banging their fists on table tops, the sound of which echoed around the splintery wooden floorboards and bare walls as if we were inside a drum. And right in the middle of it all a teenage girl was ineffectually trying to restore order, her voice barely audible above the racket. I watched the scene in horror, until someone told me they had enough help and I could go back into church if I liked. Back I went, into peace, order, warmth, light and comfort, to continue the service with excellent worship musicians, brilliant preaching and the chance to encounter God through prayer ministry. But I didn't enjoy it. I spent the rest of the service in tears, as God shared with me his heart for the poor of our church: the children. The poverty of their situation contrasted so starkly with the riches on which the adults could feed, and it broke my heart. As the years have gone on I have come to realise ever more deeply how much it breaks God's heart too.

But far more important than carpets and comfort is the scandal of the way in which our children have been denied access to the power of the Holy Spirit. That's what really hurts me. Even in overtly charismatic churches the children are told stories about Jesus, but are seldom allowed to experience his reality or power. So when I took on leadership of that children's ministry I was determined to make sure that they had all the resources, both physical and spiritual, to meet with God, grow in their faith, and mature as Spirit-filled disciples. It is out of this experience that my ministry with children over the past 15 years came to birth and has been nurtured along the way.

Up to 1997 I worked mainly within the context of Anglican local churches where my husband worked as Curate and then as Vicar. This meant that I led children's ministry Sunday by Sunday, week in week out, through Easters, Christmases, Lents and Pentecosts. But when in 1997 John was appointed

Director of Anglican Renewal Ministries, and began an itinerant ministry, my life changed too. I found more and more that I was being invited to travel and minister more widely. In particular, I found that moving to Derby meant that I struck up a friendship with Captain Alan Price, who lives two streets away from us. He provided opportunities for me to minister with him in some contexts very different from week-by-week, church-based groups. In particular it was a privilege, and a brand new experience, to work alongside him at New Wine with a group of 300 children. I discovered that the dynamics are somewhat different, although of course God's heart for the children is still the same.

So what's in this book? It has been designed to be a practical, hands-on guide for those working with children, to help them lead youngsters into an experience of the Holy Spirit, his gifts and his fruit. There is a little less theology and theory than there was in *And for Your Children*, my previous book, because I have noticed that the agenda has changed since 1994. People seem no longer to be discussing *whether* or not children should experience the Holy Spirit; they are far more concerned today with *how* children can experience him, and how leaders can help. So I talk about helping children pray out loud, speak in tongues, hear and deliver prophetic words from God, minister healing to one another and so on, and of course how they can do all this under the authority of biblical revelation.

Who is this book for? Anyone who has any input into the spiritual lives of children. The primary focus will be children's ministry leaders who have responsibility week by week for the work in local churches. However, it will be useful for church leaders, so that they can understand and actively support what the children's work is trying to do, as well as those in the church who have a heart to pray for and support the children's work, even though they may not be involved personally. And of course it will be a vital resource for parents, to whom God has given the primary responsibility for their children's nurture. Much of the material in this book has come out of my experience on Sundays with the children of the church family, but even more has come out of my role as a mother within a human, Christian family. We have sought to train our children up in the 'fear and nurture of the Lord', so that we might present them mature before Christ as his servants. This book was written to help other parents do the same.

I need to thank various people for their input into my ministry generally and this book in particular. Peter Lawrence encouraged me to begin writing back in 1993, and this book's predecessor owes its existence to him. Some friends have worked long and hard with me over the years, having faith in my vision, helping to shape it along the way, and sharing with me the joy of seeing young lives touched by the power of the Spirit. In particular Di Marples, Rachael Hansford, Hazel Wilson, Susie Jackson and Karen Hamblin deserve special thanks. Thanks too to all the children who have at one time or another been on the receiving end of my ministry, some of whom have shared stories which are included in this book. Thanks to Captain Alan Price for giving me friendship, partnership, encouragement and the opportunity to work on a broader canvas. His *Children in Renewal*[1] provides a resource complementary to this book, and working from a very similar vision. And of course my own children, Steve, Paul and Vicki, who have often been my guinea pigs, but who have shaped my vision, grasped it and begun to run with it into the next generation. And last, but by no means least, I want to thank

---

[1] Captain Alan Price CA and Liz Lunn, *Children in Renewal* (Kevin Mayhew, 2000).

my husband John for his love, support and encouragement to keep following God's leading in this ministry, and for his practical help in getting this book into print.

Above all I praise God for allowing me to share his heart for children and gifting me to do that which I have tried to do faithfully for him and for his children. I believe that there is no more vital work for the church than the discipling of its future generations, and I pray that this book will contribute towards that task.

1
The Leader

It so happened that in one of the churches in which we
worked a few years ago we had two crises at the same time.
The first was that we urgently needed more people to count
the collection after services, and the second was that there
was no one to look after the babies and toddlers in the crèche.
The leadership made a policy decision that we could not ask
just anyone to count money: they had to be people we knew
and trusted, and whose integrity and honesty were beyond
question. We would personally approach people whom we
had listed as fitting the bill. At the same time we made a general appeal at our Sunday services for anyone who could help
with the children to have a word afterwards.

Fairly quickly it dawned on us what we had done: we had
acted as though money were more important than children.
Anyone would do for them, but money had to be handled by
the 'right' people, lest something should go wrong. This attitude pervades much of the church. Consider, for example, the
human and physical geography of your church life. Could it
be that the adults, at one end of the scale, will be in the best
room, with the best musicians and the best speaker, while at

the other end the babies will be tucked away in a broom cup-
board somewhere, presided over by a few women or teenagers
who have been press-ganged into doing a shift on the rota?

This attitude also shows itself when church leaders and
people alike regard work with children as a kind of poor relation. It is often seen as a temporary stage through which people must pass before they are allowed to do something significant in the church. When I became a Christian at the age of 14
I was immediately sent off to lead a Pathfinder group (for
10–14s). This model assumes that even a brand-new Christian
will have all that is needed to work with youngsters, although
they will hopefully learn enough in the process so that one
day they will be able to graduate and lead a home group for
adults, or something equally important. While God may, of
course, call us to different areas of ministry as we travel on in
our Christian pilgrimage, it is my conviction that the church
needs children's workers who will see their ministry as a
proper ministry, and not just a stepping stone on the way to
greater things or a *real* job. I wouldn't, of course, want to ban
teenagers or new Christians from children's work. In fact
there is some evidence to suggest that one factor in the success of children's groups is involvement from slightly older
teenagers. But I would want to see them working alongside
leaders who are mature both in age and Christian discipleship.

So what sort of people might be able to lead children into
things of the Spirit? Let's begin negatively by looking at the
sorts of attitudes that won't help. First of all, a belief that the
spiritual gifts died out at the end of the apostolic age and are
therefore not for the church today might just be a bit of a hin-
drance in leading children into their use. One view held by
some Christians is that God gave supernatural gifts in order to
get the church going, but once things were established and the
Bible had been written they were no longer necessary and so

were withdrawn. This view is called 'cessationism', and it's a bit like those chokes we used to have on our cars in the old days: useful for getting you going from cold, but thereafter to be pushed in and forgotten. It leads inexorably, it seems to me, to the conclusion that all so-called manifestations of the Spirit nowadays are spurious or even satanic counterfeits. Understandably, no one would want to lead children, or anyone else, into that sort of thing. Similarly the view that the so-called 'supernatural' gifts are somewhat overrated, and we ought to be putting our energy not into tongues and prophecy but into other biblical ministries like flower-arranging, will militate against children entering into the full inheritance of the Spirit which is theirs (i.e. tongues *and* flower-arranging). Leaders must be committed to an understanding of the Spirit that involves the full biblical range of his activities in the church.

There is also a belief which regards the gifts of the Spirit as something akin to sex education: it has its right and proper use, and we personally have no problem with that, but we certainly wouldn't mention the subject to those who are too young. They'll be able to find out about things like that all in good time, when they're more grown up. Any questions now are gently deflected in a slightly patronising manner.

And third, there are those who have no theological objections as such to charismatic renewal; it's just that it scares them half to death, either because they have fantasies about what goes on in charismatic churches or because they have *seen* what goes on in charismatic churches! A leader suffering in this way will find it difficult to put the subject across convincingly, and without communicating his own terror.

It is worth considering these attitudes, because it is sometimes the case in churches that are moving into charismatic renewal that those who are most unhappy with the new direction and its manifestations are to be found in the Sunday school or children's ministry. As the services get more ravey, the guitars more loud, the spiritual gifts more frequent and the sermons more challenging, those who are threatened by this may gravitate towards the children's groups where it is safe. They have their own little empire where they can continue to teach nice Bible stories and keep the raw experience of God at arm's length. If there is a Sunday in the month when the children don't meet in groups but the whole church worships together, they stay away, claiming the need for 'a day off', and their absence from other activities such as fellowship groups is striking. Thus they can not only escape from the Spirit themselves, but also model non-involvement to the children in their care, effectively steering them out of the main flow of the church and into a calm spiritual backwater.

If this is a problem for you it may need to be tackled head-on by the church leadership. People may need to be gently challenged: their fears and hesitations must be listened to, and their concerns treated seriously and sympathetically. But at the same time they need to understand the direction in which the church is going, and if they can't lead children confidently in it, perhaps they would be better off counting the collection. This is a sensitive matter, but it does need confronting if we are to avoid creating a great chasm between the children and the rest of the church. I have visited many places where a charismatic church has attached to it a non-charismatic Sunday school. If the overall leader of the children's ministry wants a particular ethos to pervade the work, they will find it helpful to spell out from day one where they are going and what will be required of leaders.

My policy when leading children's ministry teams is to be very careful about who joins. Interested people are not immediately welcomed with open arms. They are first told about the vision for the work (as set out in Chapter 3) and asked if they can happily commit themselves at that level. They are asked at which of the other Sunday services they will worship regularly, since they will be absent from most of the main service – that's also part of the commitment, as is membership of a home group and attendance at team planning and training meetings. I try to help them see that along with the privilege of leadership goes responsibility, and that I want a commitment to remain involved for a period of time which, while not a life sentence, will give them enough time to work through the problems they may face initially. They are then given time to go away and pray and think through their calling, so that there is no sense of rush or pressure, and if they conclude that it could be right for them, they are invited to work for a few months on a probationary basis, after which there will be a review on both sides. So I have always tried to spell out very clearly what the commitment means. People won't always understand or hear what is being said, but later on I am able to say, 'Don't say I didn't warn you!' It's not that I'm looking for fully competent and experienced leaders, but I do want those who are happy to be trained in this particular ethos and model.

I also try to be as careful about the end of their ministry as I am about the beginning. For all sorts of reasons people will have to leave teams, so I have spelled out the rules for that too. I ask for a term's notice, so that we have time to seek replacements for them. (Incidentally, that is our responsibility, not theirs. I have had people trying to soften the blow of their resignation by replacing themselves with friends whom I know to be completely unsuited to the work.) A notice period also allows new people to work alongside them for a while to settle in. I ask that all the leaders of a particular sub-group do not give up at once, but stagger their going to provide continuity for the children in their care, and I do try to ensure that when people leave they move on to another area of ministry and don't just flop out and do nothing.

Ongoing envisioning and training is needed, but models for actually doing this differ considerably. In one church in the past our children's and youth workers met weekly as a home group, and no one who was not a part of that group was allowed to lead on Sundays. In other places the team might be gathered from different home groups to meet on another night of the week. But however you decide to meet, it is essential that you do meet. As well as programme planning, the team concentrates on overall policy and vision, prayer and worship, and personal growth in discipleship. In addition, members of the team are encouraged to attend outside training events that will have relevance to their ministries, and these are paid for.

While it has been necessary on a couple of occasions to lay down the law as suggested above, it has been far more our experience that within this intimate and caring environment those with hesitations about the Spirit have been led on to a much more confident place. We must at all costs, however, make sure that there is no hiding place from the Spirit among the children's work of our churches if we are to see them thrive and grow in the power of the Holy Spirit.

So what sort of positive characteristics do we want our leaders to have? Four main qualifications seem important; and we'll look at each in turn.

They must be spiritually open

First of all we need leaders who are open to the Spirit themselves, and who have a heart to see children moving in the same way. We need to break free of the traditional model of children's work outlined above, which sees it as an easy option for the spiritually not-quite-there. Instead we need those who will realise that it can be much more demanding than they'd ever dreamed, but are willing to rise to the challenge. This is not a glorified baby-sitting service so that the adults can get on uninterrupted with the real thing over in the church. We need those who will understand that they have a spiritual ministry that is part of the whole continuum of disciple-making. We need crèche workers who will pray over the babies they are soothing; toddlers' group leaders who will talk naturally about and to Jesus in the company of the youngsters with whom they're playing, and so on. It's never too early to begin, and we need to challenge the mentality of some Christians who feel they can help with the tinies because they're not spiritual enough for anything more advanced.

They must be spiritually ahead

Second, we need leaders who are both ahead of the children in their own discipleship, and therefore have things from their own experience to teach them, and at the same time willing and able to learn from them. Young children are gloriously free from our adult hang-ups about the supernatural, and so can advance quickly in the things of the Spirit if they are led in the right way. Many of them do indeed put adult Christians to shame in their levels of faith and expectancy. But conversely they can be held back by leaders who don't believe (or don't want to believe) that they can cope.

In the early days of my ministry it was common in our team home group to hear leaders protesting that the children wouldn't be able to cope with praying aloud, speaking in tongues, or whatever. What they actually meant was *they* wouldn't cope! Another common ploy was to plead age. Some leaders would say that all this was fine for the older children –

they could cope – but theirs were much too young. At the same time others were saying that theirs were too old for this stuff and we ought to restrict it to the younger group! A team leader who spots this attitude and lovingly confronts it, and who then goes on to show just how easily the children *will* cope in practice, whatever their age, can achieve much for the growth not only of the children but also the adults as well. But in the absence of such a team leader these beliefs can go unchallenged and gain general acceptance, so that children are robbed of spiritual experience with which they would be more than happy. This loss of nerve must be attacked gently but ruthlessly, or else it will rule the roost most destructively.

Another dangerous attitude is seen among people who are in favour of leading the ministry in a particular direction but would rather someone else did the dirty work for them. Part of our current job involves visiting other churches for faith-sharing weekends, and it is amazing how often we have been brought in to do various kinds of hatchet jobs that the church leaders couldn't face doing themselves. By all means invite others to give input to your children's work, but only if you are all willing to do lots of groundwork before they come, and then pick up what they've brought and carry on in the same direction.

A team leader may have to deal with the sense of threat that team members may experience as they realise that they never did any of this with their own children. They can easily be made to feel inferior, or failures, as they come to realise how much more spiritually aware their children could have been if they had known about this years ago. It may appear too late now to do anything about it, especially if their children have ceased to live as Christians. The real problem is that parents will very rarely admit this sense of shame and guilt. If they did, there could be ministry to them, and a setting free from guilt and regrets (after all, that is what the gospel is about). But it is far more common for this guilt to be buried, and rationalised with the feeling that it isn't right to give children this kind of spiritual experience just because theirs didn't get it. Children's work can be held up quite seriously if this attitude pervades, and again a sensitive team leader will need to do some gentle surgery to expose feelings about people's own past to the healing love of the group and of the Lord.

At the same time as being ahead and willing to lead the children, though, leaders must be willing to learn from the children they teach. Jesus once used a child as a visual aid, telling his disciples, 'Unless you change and become like little children, you will never enter the kingdom of heaven. Therefore, whoever humbles himself like this child is the greatest in the kingdom of heaven' (Matthew 18:3–4). While the leaders need to be ahead, they must not be superior and patronising to children, and they must be open to great spiritual insight coming through them. The humility to learn from those who will at times put us to shame is a kingdom characteristic essential in children's leaders.

Maybe a good picture would be walking a dog. Although neither of us has any great expertise in this area (John fervently believes that all animals should be where the good Lord intended them to be: in zoos), we have nevertheless picked up one crucial understanding: it is quite difficult to push a dog along on a lead. In fact, no matter how hard you try, you can't get it to go anywhere by standing behind and pushing. The knack is to go out in front and pull. In the same way you won't get children into the gifts of the Spirit by standing behind them; you've got to go out in front first. That is, after all, what 'leading' means. But, to continue the canine analogy, there will be times when your enthusiastic pet will suddenly get onto the scent of something and really go for it.

You will find yourself being pulled along, and, depending on the size and make of the dog in question, you may find it quite hard to resist. You can't push children into spiritual experience, but you can pull them, and you must be ready for those times when they'll end up pulling you.

They must be spiritually committed

Third, we need children's leaders who are called and committed to the task. The whole of the work of the church should in fact be staffed by those people who have a sense of calling, but this is especially important when it comes to those areas to do with the formation of Christian character and discipleship. By their commitment, leaders will model both the commitment of our faithful God to us, and also the commitment to the body of Christ which the true disciple will exhibit. At a time in our society when there is less commitment around to anything at all, and when many people will attend worship only when they've nothing more exciting to do, there is much that models to children those casual attitudes to church and to Christ himself which are so destructive of true discipleship.

The problem with modelling commitment as a clergy family is that people can write us off by saying, 'Well of course you're paid to be there!' Our children need other role models, and plenty of them, in whom they can see commitment to the kingdom of God as an all-consuming passion that comes at the very top of the list of priorities. Our boys knew from a very young age that they simply were not allowed to take part in sporting or uniformed group activities that conflicted with Sunday worship. There was never a hint of resentment about this; they agreed wholeheartedly with us that Jesus must come first, and that their other activities must make way for him. The secret, we are convinced, was to agree with them as early as possible that this was the policy, and to stick to it without a hint of vacillation. They would no more have expected to do something other than worship on a Sunday morning than they would have expected to do something other than go to school on a Monday. It was simply not an option. They didn't respond to friends who did play football or whatever with jealousy; they felt sorry that they hadn't got Jesus and therefore something better to do.

We've seen many young disciples diverted from their Christian commitment by their sporting or musical skills. We've even seen Christian parents trying subconsciously to live out through their children the achievements they would have liked to have been capable of themselves, and therefore pressurising them away from church. John and I were determined that we didn't want to run that risk with ours, and we believe firmly that becoming a concert pianist or winning an Olympic gold is nothing compared to the surpassing greatness of walking in the will of God. Those are not bad things to do, but they become bad if they turn into idols that divert us from wholehearted discipleship. Our children understood this and agreed completely. This attitude is a choice of will which has nothing to do with us being 'professional' Christians. Any family could adopt it if they felt it important enough.

Sadly, though, the Enemy has duped many Christian parents into colluding with him as he tries to wreck children's spiritual lives. We were once stunned to hear a speaker, addressing Christians, say that for most parents it's more important that their children get a good job than it is that they walk with the Lord. This is so obviously evident as we look around our churches and see parents fuelling their children's ambitions in the sporting, musical, dramatic or academic arenas at the expense of their spiritual growth. Polly Toynbee, writing from a secular point of view, attacks the commonly held view that we must do all we can to stimulate our children and make life fun for them:

> The anxious new parent these days from the earliest years will feel the pressing need to occupy every moment of their toddlers' lives with stimulation and entertainment ... The swimming classes, the Tumble Tots, the dancing lessons and Suzuki method violin, the Saturday morning French club, ballet and tap and the drama workshops. Wonderful, yes. But what are we saying to our kids? Life is an endless cycle of pleasure designed just for you? Everything and everyone is bent on your enjoyment, for it is the only purpose of our lives?[1]

Clearly that is not a good message to give, since they'll discover soon enough that it simply isn't true. We have so much to learn about finding our fulfilment in following Jesus, and finding our security and significance in his love. The Enemy will do all he can to dilute Christian commitment among adults and children alike, and he is not averse to using good things to keep us from the best thing. It is our conviction that we need to fight him, not help him.

Another reason why we suspect our boys are happy with this level of commitment is that they see it modelled in us. There are all sorts of ways we'd love to spend Sundays, but for the sake of the kingdom we chose to sacrifice them when we responded to God's call to ministry. We have not reached the full potential that might have been ours as, for example, golfers, but we count it a privilege to have ditched that possibility for the sake of the kingdom, and our hope and prayer is that our children will feel the same about their sacrifices. They would rather Dad didn't have to be away from home so much, of course, but they fully understand why he has chosen

---

[1] Polly Toynbee, *Radio Times,* 12–18 March 1994.

to accept a job that means he has to be (in fact they were part
of the praying and discerning process before he accepted it).
Children will spot half-heartedness a mile off, and their eye-
sight will get even sharper as they grow older. Leaders who
are not totally committed to the kingdom and the church will
lose credibility among children who are, and will model a
take-it-or-leave-it attitude to those who are not.

They must be spiritual heroes

It is a characteristic of children, and one which grows as they
do, that they need heroes. There are so many likely contenders
in the world around, and they change with alarming frequency. Footballers or other sporting giants, cartoon characters
like Bart Simpson or Eric Cartman, digital babes like Lara
Croft, or a whole galaxy of film and TV stars come and go
with great rapidity, such that I even hesitate to mention
names. By the time you finally get to read this there'll be no
telling who's the current favourite, and you'll be thinking how
quaint and nostalgic this paragraph is, and who was Eric
Cartman anyway? But the fact is that many of these heroes
are modelling the very opposite of Christian virtues, or at best
attitudes to life which leave God out altogether. Where are all
the Christian heroes? Probably the least likely object of this
type of adulation will be your vicar! If Christians don't fill the
need youngsters have for heroes, there are plenty of others
ready to come and take their place. Is it too much to expect
that some of your children's ministry leaders could fit the bill?

Many years ago, when I first wrote some of this material,
our Steve had just been picked for the school football First
Team. He'd been after this honour for a long time, slowly
working his way towards it, and the day finally arrived when
he made it! As John interrupted his work to pick him up from

the first practice and drive him home, he asked Steve if he had any heroes. Expecting some great footballing superstar to be top of the list (he could remember worshipping Danny Blanchflower himself in the past), John was surprised but gratified when without hesitation the answer came back: 'Ishmael.' If our leaders are exciting people, living out an exciting faith with a wholehearted commitment, children can't help but look up to them. Gifted leaders give birth to more gifted leaders, just as mediocre ones create mediocrity among their protegés.

It is also worth mentioning the fact here that children need same-sex heroes. Sunday schools are often staffed by women, and there is a need to see more men in children's ministry alongside women. Boys need men to look up to, and our children's work needs to have some guts to it if we are to attract men who will in turn attract boys and act as role models to them. This is especially true in an age when many children do not have a significant male presence in their homes.

So these are our four main criteria. Is all this too idealistic? Maybe you're left feeling that your set-up is so hopelessly unlike these ideals that you might as well give up now. If you are, I know just how you feel because that's what mine has always been like when we've begun. It isn't so much that people are doing a bad job – more often it's just an uninformed and un-thought-out job. So the first ingredient that needs to be injected is some vision. The team leader, who will hopefully have been envisioned by God for the task, must begin to infect others with this vision, and with his or her enthusiasm for it. If God truly has called you to leadership, and given you a vision to work with, he will not have called you in isolation; he will also have been at work in the hearts of others. My experience, which was more or less the same in each of our different parishes, was that three things began to happen as the vision was spread around.

The first is that people will get out of the way. Sometimes this is a painful and negative experience for all concerned, but more often it is with a sigh of relief that some who have ministered faithfully for years if not decades will hand on the baton to the next phase of leadership. They had thought that children's work was a life sentence, but now they find they can be released into something new. It seems to be the case that those who go gladly will find their way into another area of ministry and become contented there, while those who try to hang on when God is telling them it's time to go will become the malcontents who lose all sense of Christian identity along with their job title. It is the fault of the church that they have been allowed to find their status in their job, and it is terribly sad when they go angrily and bitterly, feeling that they no longer have a place in the church now that 'their' job has been taken away from them. This ought to be the exception, though, and your call will be confirmed to you as you see the way opening up before you.

The second thing to happen, and perhaps the rarest, is that some of the existing team will grasp your vision and run with it. God's work in their hearts will have been to cause discontent, as they have become more and more unhappy with the way things are, while not really knowing what on earth to do about it. God will have been forming questions in their minds, and they will be ready and enthusiastic when you come along with some answers. Rather than wanting to leave the team, they will be hungry to learn from the new leader, although at times they will feel a bit insecure and want to revert to the older, safer ways. They may need reminding of the discontent they feel, but in a way which helps them to understand that you are building on the past, not writing it off and reversing it.

Third, God will have been at work in others, putting on their hearts a call to join you in your new ministry. It may be rather incoherent at present, but like the sheep of Jesus' analogy they will hear your voice and respond by following you. In particular, you will begin to identify those who are still quite young but who may have a ministry with children awaiting them. Your structures need to be capable of including them in appropriate ways that will allow them to experience ministry and also to receive further training and envisioning from you.

It has never been easy rounding up a new team of workers, but it has never been impossible either. If you find yourself truly alone, with no evidence that God is working on others alongside you, it might be right to begin to ask questions about your own call, whether its time has yet come, or whether it might be a call to work alongside others for a while rather than take on overall leadership. If God really wants your children's ministry to go places, he'll set it up for you. So begin to pray first of all for a vision, second for the space to work it out, and third for those who will work with you. Realise that it'll take time to mould a team together. Rejoice over minor triumphs, reflect on and learn from major disasters, and build one another up in love. You and the Spirit between you can make a pretty good team!

2

Children in the Kingdom?

'Children are the church of tomorrow' is a commonly heard statement, but while this is usually supposed to be well meaning, when you stop and think about it, it's actually demeaning. It implies that children are not yet members of the church, but that if we play our cards right they might be one day. Just what is the place of children with regard to the church and to the kingdom? Are they 'in' or 'out', and on what criteria do we decide?

While this is an important question to ask, it takes on even more significance as soon as you begin to talk about the work of the Holy Spirit. For 15 years I ran children's ministries where the Holy Spirit was welcomed to bring his charismatic gifts, where children regularly prayed, out loud in groups, for one another in prayer ministry, and sometimes in tongues – all within the safety of the Anglican womb in which I had been nurtured as a young Christian. But more recently, as my husband has moved from parish to itinerant ministry, I too have begun to work over a much wider area, and in particular within a much broader range of denominations. Again and again, when I visit different churches or speak at conferences,

I am asked one question: how can you pray for children to move in the fullness of the Holy Spirit when they might not yet be 'saved'? As an Anglican I would have had a simple answer to this question, but lately I have needed to explore it more deeply. Just where are children in relation to God, and therefore to the Holy Spirit?

The answer is that it depends, or appears to depend, on what brand of Christian you ask. In particular you may get three different answers from those who adhere to three different positions, which for the sake of simplicity I will call the 'Baptist', the 'Anglican' and the 'New Church'. While not every Baptist would be a fully signed-up follower of the particular understanding I shall call 'Baptist', any more than all Anglicans or New Church members would of theirs, the praxis and liturgy of each of these three streams do betray their own theological position, even if not everyone has fully thought it out. I shall therefore keep the terms safely in inverted commas when they refer to each viewpoint.

In the Baptist denomination children tend to be treated as though they were outside the kingdom and need to be won into it. The normal route to membership is via believers' baptism, which rarely happens before teenage years at the earliest. This sacrament can only rightly be administered to those who have made a conscious 'adult' declaration of faith, with a certain degree of understanding of what it is they have committed themselves to. Children are 'dedicated' at birth, but this is not generally thought to include them as church members. Rather it expresses the hope that they will grow into faith in the future; there is no understanding that in some way they already have faith. The hope is that they will grow up and 'become Christians' such that they can undergo baptism as adults, and subsequently be received into membership, although they may, paradoxically, be allowed to take communion before baptism and membership if they are judged to have had a saving experience of Christ.

On the other hand those churches holding the 'Anglican' view and happy to practise infant baptism have a different understanding. Children are basically included rather than excluded, and the prayer and desire of the church is not that they will one day opt in, but rather that they won't one day opt out. A conversion experience is not seen as essential if the child's parents are actively training him or her in the ways of the Lord (although the move from family faith to personal faith does need to be made in later years).

A picture often used to explain this is that of the Israelites crossing the Red Sea. No doubt there were among their number on that day children of all ages, as well as adults. Some would have toddled through the gap in the waters, some would have been carried in their parents' arms, and some, no doubt, would have slept peacefully through the whole thing, blissfully unaware of the momentous event that God was causing to happen for them. Yet all would have been 'saved' as they reached dry land on the other side, free of the Egyptian threat. To suggest that they were not really saved unless they consciously went through a repeat performance would simply not be true, although it would presumably be possible for them at any stage to get into a boat, cross back the other way, and hand themselves back into slavery. Thus, the argument goes, those children whose parents have 'carried' them into the kingdom, and who are helping them to live out that life of freedom, do not need saving again; they need help and encouragement to live life to the full in the promised land.

The 'New Church' position is even harder to define, since the term refers to a loose affiliation of networks rather than to an organisation with set doctrines and practices. But the general understanding seems to be somewhere between the two already mentioned. As far as it is possible to lump them all together, the New Churches have a theology that looks Anglican in all but infant baptism. Children are included in the kingdom – in fact Jesus said that they were a paradigm of it – but they do need to be led into the fullness of their inheritance. They will be valued in the church and encouraged to move in ministry and in spiritual gifts, and may be allowed to receive the bread and wine at communion, but paradoxically they can't be baptised until they are 'adults'. They are not treated as if they were little heathens in need of evangelising, but at the same time they are not seen as fully integrated members of the church.

This may look pretty similar in some ways to the 'Anglican' position, but the New Churches don't usually go the whole hog with Anglicanism by granting children the sacramental sign of the membership they supposedly have, and will administer baptism only to 'adults'.[1] (It is usually the case also that infant baptism is not recognised in the New Churches, and adults who join after an Anglican 'sprinkling' as babies will be urged to undergo a 'proper' baptism by immersion.)

No doubt there are other nuances of belief and practice in between these three basic positions, and you and your church will have your own understanding of the theology of children and the kingdom (at least you should have!). But all this so far implies that the children in question are those of Christian parents, and are being brought up in an environment of faith

[1] The term 'adult' used in this way is not really an indication of a particular age (policies over which may vary considerably in different churches) but is simply opposed to the term 'infant', meaning a very young child or baby who cannot possibly have any intellectual grasp of the faith.

and nurture. What of the vast majority of children in our nation, who have no such background?

Again there would be a range of beliefs here. The 'Anglican' position tends to be that they would be included rather than excluded, while the 'Baptist' position would see them as no different in essence from unsaved children of committed parents, although of course they might be at a disadvantage in that they had less of a head start from their family and church environment. But the 'New Church' idea of 'inheritance' takes a slightly different approach. If we take at face value Jesus' words in Matthew 18:1–9 and 19:13–15, the argument goes, we must believe three things: that children exemplify the humility needed to inherit the kingdom; that if someone loses their childlike innocence and humility they are in danger of losing the kingdom too; and that it is possible for people to come between children and their place in the kingdom. We have to be childlike to enter the kingdom, and while children seem to be naturally good at this, the adults to whom Jesus was speaking had specifically to change. To take on this humility would lead individuals to greatness in the kingdom, but to refuse to do so would put them in danger both of losing their own eternal life and also possibly of leading others astray from gaining theirs.

If then children by their very nature do in some way already have the kingdom in their possession, they can grow up in one of three ways. First, they may be taught to grow and value the things of God, and they may remain within his purposes and mature into adult believers. Second, they may be brought up in an environment of faith but later harden themselves and opt out. Or third, they may grow up completely ignorant of the inheritance they have because neither their parents nor anyone else close to them has ever told them about it. This would be the state of children of no Christian background, and many of them would and do lose out on their inheritance simply through ignorance and by default.

This begs another important question: at what age do they pass from being 'children' to 'adults'? If children lose their relationship with God either through ignorance or by deliberate choice, at what stage can this be said to happen? There was much debate in the past in Baptist circles about the 'age of understanding' after which children would be consigned to the fires of hell if they hadn't got their act together with God. Nobody was able to say what this age was, but many Baptist children, my husband included, grew up in terror of reaching it!

The obvious answer to this question is that there is no answer. Children vary tremendously in their development physically, intellectually and emotionally, so why should their spiritual development be any less undefined? Some, however, would want to see pointers here in the Jewish ceremony of bar mitzvah, which was supposed to mark this transition liturgically as a distinct rite of passage at about the age of twelve. Some also feel that Luke's account of Jesus' trip to the Temple at the age of twelve similarly points to somewhere around that age as an important spiritual transition point, and our experience of having had two sons make the transition to secondary school at eleven would make us want to agree broadly with this sort of age as a significant change point.

These, then, are the three basic positions: children are out until they deliberately opt in; they are in until they deliberately opt out; or they are basically in but need to be taught to value and grow up into what it is they are 'in'. So what do these positions imply about the way we minister to children, and specifically about how we might seek to introduce them to the work of the Holy Spirit?

The 'Baptist' position means that children's ministry will

fundamentally need to be an *evangelistic* ministry. The key thing is to get the children in our care to make a commitment to Christ as Lord and Saviour: unless they do so their eventual eternal salvation might be in peril, and we as leaders might end up with their blood on our hands. Whatever the spiritual state of their families, the evangelistic task is exactly the same. And of course since the gifts of the Holy Spirit are for the use of believers, it would be both wrong and pointless to expect unbelieving children to experience them. The job of Christian parents in all this is exactly the same: to bring up our children so that they will one day want to opt in.

The 'Anglican' position, on the other hand, implies not an evangelistic but a *nurturing* task for children's ministry. They belong to God because they are included in their parents' family faith, and they can therefore safely be treated as though they were Christians, and helped to grow in faith so that it becomes more and more an attractive thing which they will one day want to take on personally. The Holy Spirit can and should be active in their lives, and we should expect them to be experiencing and growing in his gifts. Young children without Christian nurture or background in the home would generally be included on a level footing with the others. Our work with such 'unchurched' children is not to evangelise them in the sense of calling them to repent or fear the eternal frying pan, but rather to tell them the good news that they are already loved and accepted by God, and help them to get to know better the friend and Lord who has them in his loving care.

The 'New Church' practice lies, as does its theology, somewhere between these two positions, although much closer to the 'Anglican' end of the spectrum. Children would be welcomed, and might be expected to experience the power of the Holy Spirit, but would need to be taught to value personally

their welcome by God. Some would say that the dedication of
a child to God by its parents would give the child some kind
of a spiritual head-start, but *growth* into his or her inheritance
would be the key emphasis. Those who hold this position
might criticise Anglicans for their concept of 'family faith',
and certainly for baptising infants, but they might also regard
as a bit harsh the 'Baptist' treatment of all children as basically unsaved until they had made a commitment. Many would
see this as directly contrary to the way Jesus appeared to view
children.

So, having summarised these different understandings of
the place of children before God, is there anything we can do
to reconcile them? First of all, very few Christians would
want to deny the possibility of children having an experience
of Christ at an early age, whether before or after baptism.
Whether or not this is expected to be the norm, it seems clear
that it can happen, and all would hope that it would happen. It
is surely the task of children's leaders to 'introduce' children
to their heavenly Father, however we might view their relationship with him before that point. Second, it may be less
helpful to draw a great distinction between the two extremes
of evangelising and nurturing, and more appropriate to think
in terms of leading children on in faith, whether this is seen to
be before or after conversion. The 'inheritance' language of
the New Churches is again helpful here. And while I'll go on
to argue that this leading on is best done by parents within a
family, there will be many children who will need to have sur-
rogate spiritual families in order that they become aware of
God and his place in their lives.

Third, most of us would I hope agree that whether or not
we see the task of children's ministry as primarily evangelistic, we would not want to exclude careful ongoing nurture as a
part of the package. I was absolutely appalled at a conference

to hear the story of a four-year-old boy who had turned up for the first time to an evangelistic children's club, and then was tragically killed in a road accident a few days later. 'At least', said the speaker triumphantly, 'he had heard the gospel before he died.' The sense was that the team had done their duty in presenting the Christian faith, and so were free of any further responsibility. I was longing to stick my hand up and ask some questions about the theology implied by this shocking statement. Where did they think the child had gone for eternity? Was that any different from where he might have gone had he not heard their presentation of the gospel? Is the eternal salvation of four-year-old children by their loving heavenly Father *really* dependent solely on whether or not they have had the gospel explained to them? And isn't some kind of a response usually required? The school of thought that sees Christian ministry as simply presenting the gospel far and wide so that the blood of those who hear will not be on their hands seems to me a cruel parody of the task left to us by Jesus. The tasks of evangelism and nurture must go hand in hand. One of the reasons why so many teenagers leave the church (I shall tell you some other reasons later) is because since a very young age all that has been asked of them is to give their lives to Jesus, week in, week out. Once they've done that they're safely in, and nothing more challenging is ever required of them, except to hear the gospel again the following week.

I have tried to be as fair as I can to these different theological positions, but I do need to come clean at this point in terms of my own position, and the viewpoint from which this book has been written. It won't surprise you to know that I am a thoroughly convinced 'Anglican'. I believe that children are included in the kingdom by default, and that if their parents or others close to them are actively wanting, hoping and praying for them to be, they can be included in a covenant relationship with God, in which they are helped to grow to adult maturity. As an Anglican I am happy that such children are baptised,[2] since there seems little point in refusing to allow children the initiation ceremony into something to which we believe they already belong ('You can be a Brownie, come to meetings, join in the games, take badges and come on camps, but you can't jump over the toadstool until you're grown up'). Children of Christian parents have, I believe, a relationship with Jesus already, and they have it because their parents are giving it to them. Children of non-Christian parents also have a relationship with Jesus, which they don't know about yet. Maybe you'd want to call it a 'potential' relationship, although that is of course true for adult non-Christians. I see the job of children's ministry in a church, therefore, being either to back up the parents' work by encouraging the children to grow in this relationship, or to give children the information they're not getting from parents. They may, of course, subsequently opt out of living the Christian life, in which case their baptism won't be of much help to them. The fact that you once jumped over a toadstool is worth very little if you have ceased to live as a Brownie or believe in the principles of Browniehood.

I hold this position, I think, for three reasons. The first is that I have always been an Anglican, and so I have imbibed this theology with my mother's milk. If we're honest many of

---

[2] The whole question of infant baptism policy in the Anglican Church is a minefield, and it is perhaps due to the pastoral mess we've made of it that other churches like the New Churches won't touch it with a bargepole. Nevertheless I feel that the theology stands, and the pastoral practice needs to be brought into line. See Colin Buchanan, *Infant Baptism and the Gospel* (DLT, 1993).

our theological convictions do come from the culture in which we've been nurtured and taught, and there is nothing wrong with that, as long as we take them out and examine them more thoughtfully from time to time. Second, I find no incompatibility between this view and Scripture, which of course is the acid test, although it is possible for Scripture to be interpreted in different ways by different people – we simply wouldn't have denominations or viewpoints if that weren't true. But the third and strongest reason for my conviction that children do have a relationship with God is that of raw experience. Let me illustrate what I mean from a Bible story – that of the council of Jerusalem in Acts 15. There was a vital point at issue: could Gentiles become Christians, or did they first have to undergo circumcision and become properly Jewish? So vital was this question that the leaders of the church gathered in council to thrash it out.

Since the first followers of Jesus were almost all from within the Jewish nation, the presupposition of the group was that God wanted to keep it in the family. Gentiles could become Christians, but first they had to join God's chosen people the Jews. But as the council progressed, something happened to change the minds of the leaders, and Gentiles were welcomed after all – a decision that has profound implications for the church today, and particularly for the men in the church!

So what made the difference? Quite simply, they heard a report of an incident where God had done something that broke their rules. In the middle of a sermon, without so much as a by-your-leave or thank you, he had poured out his Holy Spirit on a bunch of non-Jews, given them the gift of tongues, and opened their mouths in praise and worship, pretty much as he had with the first disciples on the Day of Pentecost. Hearing about this direct experience of God made the leaders change their theology, but it was OK because James, who was chairing the meeting, turned to his Bible and found that God's plan to welcome everyone had been there all along. It was just that their 'denominational' presuppositions had made them filter out what the Scriptures actually said, until God broke in dramatically to show them the truth.

I think there are clear parallels between this incident and the issue we are discussing in this chapter. For me, the question of whether or not children are 'saved' is completely bypassed because I have seen again and again that God has poured out his Spirit on them, gifting them in ways that look exactly like adult manifestations of the same gifts. 'Can anyone keep these people from being baptised with water?' asked Peter as he watched those whom the church had regarded as 'outside' being shown to be 'inside' as far as God was concerned. 'They have received the Holy Spirit just as we have.' In the same way it seems to me from empirical observation that the Father is pleased to pour out his Spirit on even the youngest of children. Who then can keep them from being welcomed into the church as full members of the kingdom of God?

That's where I stand, but of course it is not true to say that this book will be of no use to you if you disagree! My burning desire is to see children's ministry helping children to receive from their heavenly Father all that he has for them, and not just laying again and again foundations of repentance. I long to see them filled with the Spirit, moving in his gifts and growing in his fruit. If you believe they have to undergo a conversion or somehow make a commitment first, that's no problem: get them to do it, and then carry on with everything else in this book!

3

A Vision for Children's Work

There is a fascinating moment early in Mark's Gospel when
Jesus, who has risen early to go and pray, is found by his disciples. 'Everyone is looking for you!' they anxiously tell him.
Jesus replies, 'Let us go somewhere else – to the nearby vil-
lages – so that I can preach there also. That is why I have
come' (Mark 1:35–38). As a busy clergy family we have
drawn great encouragement from these verses over the years.
Jesus has no problem at all with saying 'no' to one pressure
because he already knows what he must say 'yes' to.

What makes this difference? The key is *vision*. I said in the
introduction that this book is about the whole work of the
Holy Spirit with children. One of the objections raised against
charismatic renewal in the church is that it is all froth with no
depth or substance to it, and sadly this accusation has been
true in some cases. Therefore it is important to reiterate that
my vision for this book is not just that it will help children to
be charismatic; rather it's about helping them to be disciples.
You can (and sadly some adults do) speak in tongues as much
as you like and still have a rebellious spirit and a heart turned
away from God. The gifts of the Spirit are important, but only

41

in a context of the sort of sanctification that flows out of obedience.

If, as I have argued, children should be regarded as 'in'
rather than 'out', and if the church is the context in which
their ongoing discipling into the fullness of the Spirit is to
take place, it is important that everyone has agreed standards
and expectations, and that all can work together. In other
words we need a common vision.[1] Over the years I have
found it helpful to set out clearly my vision for children's
ministry, for several reasons.

First, we need constantly to remind ourselves what we're
here for. This is true of the whole ministry of local churches,
and the church of which John was Vicar had both a vision
statement and a 'strap-line' (a catchphrase or motto that said
in seven words why we thought we were there). The vision
statement fitted neatly (along with our church logo) onto a
piece of A5 paper, and we put it wherever we could: onto our
weekly notice-sheet, magazine and so on. The shorter strap-
line went in even more places, like the front cover of service
books and on our letterheads and business cards. Thus we
were always reminded what it was we were trying to do.

Second, a vision statement of some kind is useful for
checking out whether we are actually doing what we are supposed to be doing. If we have a clear target at which to aim, it
helps us to stay pointing in the right direction. So we didn't
run the church by responding to the many new ideas and
demands that plopped through the letter box each week, or the
multitude of plans or programmes that promised to revolu-
tionise us, our worship, our pastoral care or whatever. Rather
we evaluated new ideas according to whether or not they

[1] See J. Leach, *Visionary Leadership in the Local Church* (Grove, 1997) for
a brief account of the subject of vision.

would help us towards the fulfilment of our vision. It was also very helpful in uncluttering the church to say of some events or organisations that they weren't in line with the vision, so they had to go. Since the church council members were collectively responsible for the vision statement, they could (and usually did) all agree when some axing had to be done.

And third, a clear vision can be clearly communicated. In our children's ministry we were able to tell parents, particularly new ones, what we would be doing with their children if they left them in our care, and why. We could say the same to the church leadership and so be helpfully accountable to them, and, perhaps most important of all, we could tell prospective workers in our teams what we were about, and what would be expected of them. I began with a whole chapter about leaders, so I won't repeat it here, but it is important to be able to let new members know what they're in for.

So here is my vision. It's not important, of course, that you work with my vision, but it is vital that you work with yours. You can't import someone else's vision wholesale, but you can use it as a helpful basis for writing your own. Maybe mine will be helpful as you do this.[2]

It's based around four 'R's: *Relationship, Resourcing, Relevance* and *Really good*. Each of these has two statements, which I'll set out and unpack.

Children's Ministry Vision Statement

Relationship
Children have a relationship with God.
They have an Enemy who is trying to spoil it.

---

[2] For a useful group session designed to help leaders work towards articulating a vision, see Alan Price's *Children in Renewal* (Kevin Mayhew, 2000), pp.13ff.

Resourcing

Children need to grow intellectually in knowing about God.
They need to grow experientially in knowing God.

Relevance

Children's ministry should invest for the future.
It should have application now.

Really good

Children's ministry should be fun.
It should have quality.

Relationship

Children have a relationship with God

In the second chapter we discussed the place of children with
respect to the kingdom of God, and depending upon your
point of view you may have agreed or not with the conclusions I reached and the point of view from which this book is
written. I believe that whether or not they know it, children
have a relationship with God. Some will need telling about it,
but others will need strengthening in it. Our job therefore is
one of both evangelism and nurture: to ensure that children
enter into their inheritance as members of the kingdom, and to
help them grow up in the things of the Spirit.

They have an Enemy who is trying to spoil it

Unfortunately there is another side to this relationship with
God, and an Enemy in the form of the devil who will do all he
can to wreck it, terminally if possible. There is a battle on for
the lives of our children and youngsters, and we want God to
win. What's more, the battle is hotting up. You only have to
watch the media, listen to music, visit schools or browse

through toyshops to see that evil and occultism are coming more and more into the light of day. There is much more exposure to overt evil than we have known before, and the statistics suggest that the Enemy is gaining ground among children and youth.

A few years ago we were shocked by the torture and murder of two-year-old Jamie Bulger by two ten-year-olds. This is an extreme example, but the epidemic of juvenile crime and the steady loss of 400 youngsters each week from the church in this country shows that we have some work to do. The Enemy is slaughtering the spiritual life of children and teens in a way that is far more dramatic than any terrorist bomb. What's more, he doesn't mind how early he gets them, while in the church we have thought and taught that the supernatural weapons the Spirit gives us for warfare are only for those grown up enough to understand them. Our task, as I'll go on to explain, is to see that our children are fully resourced to fight back.

But what about the accusations of indoctrination that are so often thrown at the evangelical wing of the church? Isn't it akin to brainwashing to evangelise children, who are gullible and idealistic and easy prey for persuasion? And getting them into all this weird stuff about the Holy Spirit when they're too young to argue back is surely highly dangerous?

Brainwashing and indoctrination? Hold on a moment! Just look around at who and what else are seeking to influence our children's minds. Does the Enemy have any qualms about indoctrinating our children's minds with materialism or rebellion or violence or the occult? No; he'll use whatever he can on children from as early as he can to bend them towards his way, the way that leads to destruction both now and for eternity. Why then should we hesitate to lead our children into the ways of righteousness and the things of God? This is nothing less than a satanically inspired loss of nerve on the part of the church, and we need to unmask it as such as quickly as we can. If we don't believe that the gospel is the only thing that will benefit and bless our children, and if we don't believe that it is only a mass turning to Christ that will bring any hope to our broken world, then why on earth do we bother at all? Satan has no problem whatsoever with brainwashing our children, and the church, duped by the liberal agenda of the culture, just lets him get on with it in the name of tolerance and freedom of thought. This is a class one scandal, and this book is about how we fight it. If their relationship with God is to see the light of day and survive, children need all the help and equipment they can get.

Resourcing

We'll take the next two statements together:

Children need to grow intellectually in knowing about God, and they need to grow experientially in knowing God.

It is important to understand that both these dimensions of growth need to be involved in the discipling of children (as they do with that of adults), because it is possible to know God in different ways. The French have two words that mean 'to know'. *Savoir* means to know about, to have factual information, and part of the children's growth will mean that they learn more and more about the facts of the gospel, about Jesus and the kingdom. This is about their knowledge and use of the Bible, and this is where Sunday schools have traditionally been strong, and where in these days of increasing secularisation there is more need than ever before. Schools and homes are providing less and less in terms of what used to be called 'religious knowledge' (at least *Christian* religious knowledge

– many children today know far more about the mosque and the gurdwara than they do about the church), and fewer and fewer children are in touch with churches to gain that information. Our children's ministry has an important informing role to a generation where ignorance is rife, and this role must never be decried.

But there is more to 'knowing' than just possessing facts. The French also talk in terms of *connaître*, which is about a personal acquaintance with someone. Our children need not just an intellectual knowledge of Jesus, but also an experiential relationship with him. This is where the partnership of word and Spirit is so important. We do want our children to know Bible stories, and to grow to be more like the God of whom they read. But we want them also to have experiences of God which touch their emotions and bodies as well as their minds. Our vision is to see children trained into a biblical knowledge of Jesus and the gospel, *and* an experiential grasping of their relationship with him. They will be taught from Scripture about the spiritual battle in which they're caught up, and they will be trained in the use of the supernatural weapons of warfare, both defensive and offensive.

Why is experiential as well as intellectual knowledge so important? Because it is one thing to cast doubt on someone's beliefs, but quite another to try to talk them out of their experiences. The story of the blind man in John 9 illustrates this. It was easy for the authorities to tie him up in knots over his theology. Yes, it might have helped if he had had a better knowledge of who Jesus was, but the real clincher as far as he was concerned was his experience: 'One thing I do know. I was blind but now I see!' (John 9:25). Children who have seen miraculous healing on Sunday in church (and who may even have been the ones praying for or receiving it) will be harder to convince at school the next day that God doesn't exist. The generation we are now seeing abandon the church is the result of a previous generation which had some head knowledge but little experience of God.

A few years ago Anglican Renewal Ministries ran a conference called 'Empowering Youth', which began with a service of lament for all the children and young people who had been lost from the church over the past 20 years. This service, which became known as the 'Lentil Liturgy', provided a heart-breaking visual aid: mung beans, one for each lost youngster, were poured out on the altar of the church. There were 907,000 of them, and they filled 38 milk bottles and took nearly 15 minutes to pour out as the procession moved relentlessly forward to the sound of solemn music and verses from Lamentations about the lost children. It was a tremendously moving piece of liturgy, and a sober place to begin a youth work conference.

Why this tragic waste? One of the reasons is what I call the 'Father Christmas Syndrome'. When we were little our parents told us about this man in a red coat and boots who crept down the chimney once a year and left presents for us. It was a lovely story, but inevitably the time came when we began to ask questions. John can remember clearly asking his mum how Father Christmas would be able to get down the chimney now that the fireplace had been closed up and central heating fitted. His mum told him that Santa moved with the times and nowadays he came in through the back door. This was satisfying for a while, but once the questions begin, they have a way of continuing. 'Mum, how does he get in the back door, because you lock it up every night?'

'Well, we don't lock it up on Christmas night, so he can get in.'

This was fine for another year or two, but by now John's young mind had become corrupted. 'Mum, if there is one night in the year when everyone leaves their back doors unlocked, why don't burglars take advantage of it, especially as there are piles of goodies everywhere?'

By now Mum was on the run. 'Because all the burglars in the world have an agreement among themselves that they won't do any burgling on Christmas night.' In the end John could cope with this no longer and found out the awful truth, a sadder but wiser little man.

This same process goes on in the churches of our land, and is similarly responsible for mass disillusionment and deserting of the church during adolescence. We tell our children in Sunday schools all sorts of wonderful stories of a Jesus who heals the sick, works miracles, changes lives and all the rest of it, but inevitably the time comes when there is questioning. Adolescents, as we shall see later, need above all to question everything to get to the reality, or otherwise, of what they've been told. Suddenly children's ministry leaders, like John's mum, have to do some pretty quick and convoluted thinking in order to explain why Jesus never seems to do very much nowadays: like believing in Father Christmas, teenagers simply grow out of it when they find no physical evidence that any of it is true. It does seem to be the case that the churches holding on to teenagers tend to be those that help them into a supernatural experience of the Spirit of God to go with their information about him. I can honestly say that in our parish teenage drop-off was almost totally eliminated. The few who did go almost all went because they considered the demands of Jesus on them too radical, and some of them returned in later years.

I once heard a speaker from an organisation that helped to extricate teenagers from involvement with the occult. He said that a very high proportion of the teenagers he had dealings with were from evangelical Christian backgrounds, and his slant on this was that their Sunday school stories had given them a taste for the spiritual realm, but ultimately couldn't deliver the goods, forcing them to look elsewhere. Information is great, but the hard facts about traditional Sunday school methods prove that it hasn't been enough. So often young people are told that the armour and weapons God has provided don't really exist, or at best they have them issued when the battle has already been raging for years. No wonder there are so few left to claim them.

Relevance

Children's ministry should invest for the future

I'm convinced that society is the worse for lack of obedience and the fruit of the Spirit among its members, and that God has provided childhood as a time to learn right values and character, and that families are the place to teach them. We have in our hands for a few precious years some young lives, and they have the potential of being those who are special to God in his redemptive work in the world as he brings in his kingdom. At the moment, they're immature, unformed, noisy and fickle, but by doing what we can to bring them closer to God, we hope to help build into them Christian virtues that will be salt and light in our dark and rotten world. We are very conscious of the privilege of children's ministry, and hope and pray that some of those who have been under our care will grow up to be great spiritual leaders in the nation. We want to see them knowing God better in both the ways mentioned above, and growing more and more effective in ministering for him.

This is not an uncommon aim, you may think, among children's workers, but it needs to go side by side with the second statement:

Children's ministry should have application now

Most Sunday schools see their work as investing for the future, but few seem to manage to make a more immediate impact. My lasting impression of my Sunday school years is that I was given lots of information that I would one day find useful, when I grew up and became a *proper* Christian and church member. My job was to file it away in case I ever needed to find it. In reaction to this, I am now concerned to make what I teach relevant when the children go home for Sunday lunch, or are in school the next morning.

Often the problem here is one of application. Bible stories are left hanging in mid air, with no indication given of how they might actually impact the children's lives. Jesus becomes a very grown-up person, but not one who will be beside them in the night when they have a bad dream, or in the classroom when their friends are laughing at them. Sometimes we need to give practical help to children to encourage them to work out for themselves what it is they've learned.

On one occasion we were teaching on the need to be articulate about Jesus, as a prelude to some work on sharing our faith. I could have just told a Bible story about a blind man or something, and ended with the injunction for the children to spread the word themselves, but I chose instead a more creative way of handling it. The children were asked to brainstorm as many names of Jesus as they could think of: King, Good Shepherd, the Vine, the Bread of Life and so on. Then they were told to be still and quiet for a moment; I invited the Spirit to come on them, and they had to decide which *one* of these titles was their favourite. Then the whole group went on to construct a banner, which had 'Jesus' written in huge letters across the middle, and round the edge lots of little felt pictures which each child had done to illustrate their particular favourite: a crown, a crook, a bunch of grapes, a loaf or whatever.

When it was finished, the banner was taken and hung up in the church itself, where the adults met. The grown-ups were told about the making of the banner and encouraged to find an opportunity to ask one of the children, 'Which is your little bit?' This led on to conversations about why they had chosen that particular image of Jesus, what it meant to them and so on. Thus the children were not just told they should talk about Jesus – they were given practical help to begin to do so immediately.

This had other advantages: not only did it avoid the temptation to store the information away until they were 'proper Christians' later on and could act on it, it also removed the guilt with which most church members are weighed down as they listen to sermon after sermon and do absolutely nothing in response.[3] Preachers and teachers may berate their congregations for their lack of action, and sometimes they may do so with justification, but often they could give a lot more help by making a response easier. Growth and learning become something that actually works, now, and a much more positive attitude to the whole process is engendered.

So our vision is to see children grow, in their closeness to God and in their effectiveness against evil, in a way that has relevance for the present as well as the future. We are aware of their limitations at the moment, but concerned to see them reach greater maturity.

Really good!

Our last 'R' tells us not what our children's work must do, but what it must be like.

---

[3] J. Leach, *Responding to Preaching* (Grove, 1997) has some practical suggestions about expecting and getting response.

Children's ministry should be fun

Many of us adults have memories of enduring Sunday school rather than enjoying it. Many of us only kept going out of duty, or because our parents kept taking us out of duty. Nowadays the concept of duty is virtually dead, and if we are to keep children coming back week by week for more, we will have to make them want to.

There is so much competition, and we seldom hear children being enjoined to go out into all the world and spread the good news that there is a mini-rugby club in the park on Sunday mornings, and then to compel people to come in. In fact there's a hefty waiting list, because children really do want to join. My aim has always been to create children's work that grows and gains a reputation far and wide. The only way to do this is to make it fun.

On one occasion the leader of a uniformed group, no doubt to impress us with his piety, was reassuring us that the children in his care didn't just mess around on all this secular stuff like knots and British Bulldog. 'We can be quiet and serious too,' he said. This is exactly the image that 'church' has with those who seldom go: there is fun, and then there is religion, and never the twain shall meet. Our vision is to make religion fun.

So we teach through games. On one occasion one of our team was doing some work with the younger children on 'families'. She asked them to think of as many things as they could that went on in families. They wrote a long list, which included nice things like cuddling, as well as others like fighting, divorce, jealousy and so on. Next they blew up loads of balloons and wrote on each of them one word from the list. Then they all went outside, where the weather was conveniently blustery, and, as an act of prayer, simply let go of all the balloons they didn't want in their families, and watched as they were blown away. No doubt there were a few surprised Sunday morning gardeners around the parish wondering where this balloon had come from and why it should have 'People needing to phone Childline' written on it, but for the children it was a tremendous piece of teaching. This kind of divergent thinking on the part of the leaders is a vital ingredient in turning 'religion' into 'fun'.[4]

I have found that one important way of helping to do this is to ban from our vocabulary school-type terminology. While for most children the thought of school doesn't hold quite the terrors it might have done for previous generations, it may still not be the word they would associate most strongly with fun. So I have never called the ministries for which I have been responsible 'Sunday school', and I have never referred to teachers, classes, lessons or homework. All that has to do with what the children *have* to do during the rest of the week; the last thing we want to do is to suggest that what happens on Sunday is just more of the same. So instead of the above, we talk about 'leaders', 'groups', 'sessions' and 'things to do at home'.

Other things too can add to the fun element. Mobility is one of them. Children are not required to sit still and listen all the time while an adult talks to them. Quite the opposite in fact: we often began with a few minutes of aerobics to a praise tape. Colour is another. The leaders often chose their most colourful clothes for a Sunday morning, because it all created the right atmosphere. And because we were an Anglican church, we often invited the congregation, including children, to dress up in the liturgical colour of the day. The vicar does, so why not them? So people, warned the week before, turned

---

[4] See the helpful *Children's Ministry* series by Kingsway for practical suggestions on bringing children's ministry alive through creativity.

up in red on Pentecost Sunday, purple for Advent and so on.
All in all, everything we do should point to the fact that you
really can be serious and have fun at the same time.

Children's ministry should have quality

The musicians, the OHP slides, the room in which we meet,
the leaders, even the little things we make to take home at the
end should be the best we can make them. Children enjoy
making things, but they will not be proud of those they know
were slung together from materials the leaders had scraped
together. Once we wanted to make a picture for the children to
take home as a memory aid for a Bible verse. Well in advance
we asked one of the best artists in the church to come up with
something, and he drew a line picture which we then photo-
copied (discarding the ones that were faint or had black blobs
of toner on them). The children were then invited to bring in a
favourite photo of themselves, and they coloured and decor-
ated their sheets and stuck their photo in the middle. The finished article had their name, a large pair of outstretched hands
holding their picture, and the words of Isaiah 49:16: 'I have
written your name on the palms of my hands.' This master-
piece remained on our son Steve's bedroom wall for months,
as a daily reminder of God's faithfulness to him personally.

Let's not give children bits of junk to take home each week.
They can tell quality when they see it, and they'll value it
much more.

Quality is not just valued by children: it values them. It tells
them that they are important to the church; that they aren't
just to be given the fag-end of its human and material
resources. Whether or not we like it, they are used to high
quality in other areas. They watch videos, not film-strips.
Their schools are full of brightly coloured books with lots of
pictures. They listen to their own mini-disks and CDs. We've

got to compete if we're to keep them. Extra creativity, extra time, even a bit extra on the budget will repay our investment in terms of growth among our children.

So *Relationship:* with God, but with the devil trying to interfere. *Resourcing:* helping children to grow in their closeness to God and their effectiveness in taking their stand against evil, and giving them everything God has got to help them, now, when they need it most. *Relevance:* for the future but for now too, and children's ministry that is *Really good* to go to and really good in quality.

That, or something like it, is what we're trying to do. But what do we actually teach? Having set out some principles, I'll now move on to being much more practical. We'll look at a strategy for teaching and learning, and then we'll begin, as all good enterprises should, with prayer.

4

The Learning Process

So you've got your vision. That's great – it's a very good start – but there is so much more. The mere fact that you can see in your mind's eye something better does not of itself get you there. Moses could no doubt visualise a land flowing with milk and honey, but he still had to spend 40 hard years getting there before he could see the reality, and even then he never quite made it in. Having decided I wanted a children's ministry based around the four 'R's I then had to make it happen, and like Moses I think I'd say that although we got pretty close at times we never fully arrived. So how do we turn vision into reality and make dreams come true? This chapter is about strategy, and it is every bit as important as the last.

I trained as a primary school teacher, and I spent six years in normal class teaching, but when returning to work after having a family I made a career change and began working with special needs children within mainstream schools, particularly those who were experiencing varying degrees of difficulty with reading, writing and spelling. I had a set amount of time with each child, from a term upwards, and in consultation with others I needed to decide what was practical to expect of him or her, and how we might set about achieving our aims. As I reflected on this process during eight years in the job, I realised that some of what I was doing on a Sunday in church was pretty similar to the things I was doing at school during the week. This helped me to formulate a four-stage strategy for teaching new things to the children, and with slight variations I have found that it works for all sorts of different topics. I'll go through the process first, and then apply it in three different areas of charismatic learning.

I've called the four stages vision, small steps, practice, and integration. Let's look at them in turn.

Vision

In the last chapter we talked about having an overall vision for your children's ministry. What we are looking at now is more to do with the specific aims for this piece of learning – what the educationalists might call 'outcomes'. 'I want the children to be able to speak in tongues' is an outcome: it states what you think you could see but what you don't necessarily see yet. Your job is then to use the rest of the process to make your vision reality.

You can, of course, teach things without a clearly articulated vision, but it will be a pretty random and haphazard affair. Everything I said about large-scale vision in the last chapter applies equally to small-scale learning projects. Vision keeps us on track and helps us to see how we're doing. So for each project we would spell out clearly what we were wanting to see happen.

Another picture that might help to explain this is that of birth. Church leaders often talk about their desire to see God bringing something to birth in the life of the church, whether prayer, giving, the gifts of the Spirit or whatever. There is usually a period of gestation, where they would teach and preach on the subject in hand, until the church (or most of it) would feel ready to have a go. Then would follow a period of more intensive activity, where the issue being born took a lot of people's time and attention. But then the new thing would hopefully grow up and become a less demanding and more natural member of the family. So the question to ask under the 'vision' heading is quite simply: 'What are we trying to bring to birth here?' As I said, we'll work this out later with three practical examples.

Small steps

The bread and butter of my special needs teaching was the construction of what are called 'small steps programmes'. This approach is based on the ancient joke: 'How does an ant eat an elephant? Answer: one mouthful at a time!' Steps in a house provide a way of getting three metres up into the air to the bedroom without ever having to move your feet more than 20 centimetres. This principle can be carried over into learning situations.

At work, when faced with a particular child, I would assess the current state of progress, review the possibilities and formulate my 'vision' for what I thought we could achieve in the given timescale. Then I would break the job down into manageable steps. The task for a term, for example, might be to help a child recognise and distinguish between simple words containing 'ch' 'sh' and 'th' sounds. For the first few weeks we would work exclusively on 'ch', playing word games, tracing letters made out of sandpaper with our fingers, writing the words or putting them on the computer, and a huge variety of other activities, until I felt that they had grasped 'ch' pretty well. Then we'd move on and do the same with 'sh' words, until we had realised my 'vision' for the term.

In the same way, the seemingly huge and impossible task of getting a group of children to feel comfortable praying out loud, for example, can be broken down and tackled a bit at a time. Each step leads you inexorably upwards towards the level you're aiming for, but none on its own seems too impossible to achieve. There are lots of little encouragements along the way as each step is negotiated successfully, and confidence can be built up through these minor achievements. (See the next chapter for one way to bring this about.)

Practice

Earlier I used the illustration of birth, and those who have experienced the joys of brand-new parenthood will know that the early days centre almost totally around the new offspring. Having achieved your aim through the small steps programme you constructed, you will then need to work hard to make sure that what has been brought to birth doesn't suffer perinatal death. My school children, having mastered a new skill, needed to practise quite hard lest they forget the lessons they'd learned. So will our children at church. This will involve lots of opportunities for practice built into your programme and timetable, and a refusal to move on to other concerns until things are more firmly established and thriving. But after a while you can move on to the fourth stage.

Integration

The attention-demanding newborn baby gradually settles down and becomes just one member of the family, who will get some attention but will not necessarily dominate. In the same way, once a new skill has been acquired it will demand

less of your time and attention. It must not be totally neglected, but it should settle down and become a normal and
natural part of what you do as a group. From time to time it
will require more special attention, but mostly it will just be
there without anyone thinking very much about it. All those
weeks mastering 'ch' sounds will be forgotten as reading,
writing and spelling skills continue naturally to grow and
progress. Praying out loud, or whatever you've been working
on, will simply be one of the many things you do as a group.

This, then, is the process, and my experience, just to encourage you, is that you only really have to go through it once
with each topic with each group of children. In the next chapter I'll tell you about how we got our five-year-olds praying
out loud. By the time they reached five, prayer was fully integrated, but new children joining the group at the age of six
didn't have to go through the whole process. They were simply 'socialised' into it by the other children because it was
expected that this would be a natural thing the group would
do together. Had we seen sudden revival and been flooded by
loads of new children we might have had to repeat the exercise for their benefit, but natural and gradual growth can easily be coped with without constant revisiting. We would simply begin again with the next group of three- to four-year-
olds.

But what if it doesn't work? You might have a very clear
vision, but simply not see it fulfilled within your projected
timescale. Is the model faulty, or were you?

All sorts of things might have gone wrong. You might have
set your sights too high, not realising what a massive issue
you were facing. Conversely you might have made your
timescale too short. You might also have made your small
steps too large, so that they were still not manageable. Just as

achievements along the way bring encouragement, so failures can scupper the whole exercise, giving messages like: 'If we can't even manage this, what hope have we got of getting all the way?' These reasons, and others to do with the construction of the process, might have caused problems.

But it might be the case alternatively that the model was fine – it simply wasn't worked out properly. Leaders can lose momentum and energy, become side-tracked into a different agenda, lose their nerve at key points along the way, and either get stuck on one step for too long, or leap ahead impatiently, skipping a few vital steps in their desire to see the vision fulfilled more quickly.

And, without using this as an excuse for our own lack of skill, it nevertheless has to be said that any growth in the work of the Holy Spirit among our children will involve a spiritual battle, and often a battle of some severity. We are not just teaching kids to read; we are building for the long-term growth of the kingdom of God. Therefore we need to do so fully armed, prayerfully, and aware of the likely opposition. That is not to say we should blame every little thing that goes wrong on the devil when actually we messed up, but spiritual warfare is a factor, and some places and churches do seem to be harder to work in than others.

I don't believe, though, that any of this invalidates the model. The best way to approach it is as a learning experience for you. After a few years in children's ministry I knew pretty well what the children were capable of. Of course there was some variation in the different groups coming up each year through the system, but not that much. I learned to fine-tune the model until it worked pretty consistently, and you will need to do the same.

One final word from the world of education, where we began this chapter. There is this doctrine called 'teacher expectation and pupil behaviour', which means in lay terms that generally pupils will achieve pretty much what their teachers expect they will achieve and not a lot more. This is a well-documented phenomenon which applies every bit as much in church children's ministry as it does in school during the week. If you find yourself thinking, as you read this book, 'My kids could never do that!' then the sad fact is that you're probably right: they almost certainly won't under your leadership. But the converse is true, so stretch your faith muscles, refuse to listen to the discouraging whispers of the Enemy, and go for it. In the next chapters I'll tell you exactly how to.

5

Speaking to God

My particular church tradition is, and always has been, one that values corporate vocal extempore prayer. That isn't to say that we see no value in other sorts: indeed we try to build into our children a love for liturgy, a respect for silence, an appreciation of the use of the senses in prayer and so on, but it does seem important to all Christians, and particularly to children, that they can cope with sharing with others in prayer by praying out loud and out of their hearts.

First of all there is Jesus' teaching in Matthew 18:19 about agreeing in prayer. This suggests, at the very least, that there is special power in intercessory prayer when two people can put their wills and hearts into it together. This does seem to presume that they can hear what it is they're agreeing about. Second, it builds in some kind of accountability. When people pray silently and individually there is no way whatsoever of knowing what they're praying for, to whom they think they're praying, or even indeed if they are praying at all. Praying is a corporate activity as well as an individual one, and we pray as members of a community, so we owe it to ourselves and the community that we get it right at least some of the time. In

our Anglican services we have a point where we recite the
Creed together. This is a statement of our common beliefs,
and no one would seriously suggest that we use instead three
minutes' silence where we can all tell God individually what
we think about him! We're accountable to one another and to
the church community as a whole, and children especially
have their faith formed to some degree by correction of misunderstandings that come to light as we hear them pray.

Third, learning to pray aloud can help make God more real
to us, and our relationship with him more immediate. There
are times when we sit in silence with our family, or when we
read passages of poetry or Shakespeare to each other (not all
that many times, come to think of it, but some). But most of
the time we just chat about what's going on, what we'd like,
what we think about each other and so on. If we felt we could
only converse with one another using someone else's words, or
by silently contemplating each other, it could well have the
effect of stinting communication between us a bit. Yet many
Christians can only communicate with God via a book and
400-year-old language. If children can be taught to talk to God
naturally and easily, in the same sort of everyday language
they might use with friends or family, it can't help but make
them feel that God *is* a friend, and they *are* in his family.

And finally my observation would tell me that those who
find it hard to talk aloud *to* God tend to be those who find it
hard to talk *about* him. Teaching people to pray aloud will
have spin-offs in that they'll learn to be more vocal about
their faith and their Lord generally, and their witnessing will
be helped. So I have always worked with a policy of teaching
vocal prayer, along with other sorts, to the children in my
care. It's not the only way to pray, and it's not the be-all-and-
end-all, but Christians who become paralysed at the prospect
are not enjoying all the resources God has for them, and are

living to some degree a handicapped spiritual life.

So how do you teach children to do it, and when? The answer to the second question is easy: as soon as they can talk. Childhood, and especially early childhood, is a phase of unparalleled growth and learning, and we can cash in spiritually on this tremendous capacity. If a child can talk, he or she can talk to God. So let's begin the lesson. We'll work through the process I outlined in the last chapter in a moment, but first of all there is some ground-clearing to be done.

First, you need to forget most of what you were taught as a child. 'Hands together eyes closed' was a command designed to protect young children from distraction. But the effect it had on many of us was to tell us that prayer is something you do for a set time in a set way. If we could only pray with eyes closed and hands together, and we took seriously Paul's command in 1 Thessalonians 5:17 to 'pray continually', we'd never be able to drive, prayer-walk or, incidentally, read from a prayer-book. It's a lot more helpful if we can learn to use the 'distractions' as aids to prayer. This denial of the physical is particularly difficult for young children, who meet the world through eager senses.

Similarly the terminology we use is important. To talk to very young children about 'praying' is to introduce a concept that may be foreign to them, whereas they can relate much more easily to 'talking to God', since they already know what it is to 'talk to Mummy'. They're already halfway there. In a nutshell, cut the super-spirituality and be natural with them.

Second, plan to build in both prayer times and spontaneity. A friend of ours used to say that it is easier to pray *any time* if you've first prayed *sometime*. Building in structured times for prayer will set children free for the spur-of-the-moment prayer which treats Jesus as a friend to whom we can talk at any moment without making a big fuss about it. We were driving off on holiday on one occasion, but our excitement was marred slightly by the presence of big black clouds glowering in the sky ahead of us. Suddenly, in the middle of a conversation about nothing in particular, one of the boys said, 'Dear Lord Jesus, please make the clouds go away so we can have a good holiday. Amen.' As parents and part-time theologians we knew of course that it wasn't as easy as that, but we were surprised when, about ten minutes later, the sun broke through and Steve said, 'There you are – isn't Jesus clever!' There's no doubt that 'times when we are going to talk to Jesus' and spontaneous intercessions go hand in hand, and we must build on one and be prepared for the other.

Third, I have found it a helpful habit to insist that everyone prays every time we have a 'sometime'. This creates a climate and an expectation that everyone is involved and, more importantly, that we pray no matter how we feel – a vital lesson for adult Christians to have learned. Obviously this is most helpfully learned within the family, but it can be done in Sunday groups too. Even if youngsters don't expect to pray out loud every day at home, you can still create the culture where they know they'll have to every week at church. This is only difficult, in my experience, at the beginning. Once the habit has been established and the culture created, children will fit quite happily into it.

I still haven't answered the question about *how* to teach children to pray out loud, but I have set out some helpful preconditions. We're now ready to move on to the learning process.

Vision

So what do we want to happen? In one of our churches, one tier of the children's ministry took them from three-and-a-half to five years old. First of all, the leaders set out their vision or goal: by the time the children moved up at the age of five to the next group they should all be confident and unembarrassed about praying aloud with others. This meant that we had an 18-month period to do the job.

Small steps

We then constructed our 'small steps programme', which would gradually take the children from where they were on arrival in the group to where we wanted them to be by the time they left. The 18-month timescale was broken down into five small steps, which were worked through in small groups with one leader for every three or four children. We found this to be a very leader-intensive process, but felt it important enough to invest in to such a high degree.

Step 1

The leaders did everything. They chose a subject to pray about, prayed about it, and said 'Amen' at the end. The subject would be one that flowed wherever possible out of the teaching material of that particular day. After a while the children learned to join in with the 'Amen'! The subjects for prayer were simple and familiar, and the leaders modelled short, jargon-free prayers.

Step 2

The leaders then asked the children to repeat the prayers phrase by phrase after them, until they could do so without any problems. This and the 'Amen' from Step 1 took them past an important landmark which many adult Christians have never passed: they broke the 'sound barrier' and heard their own voices talking to God. This major barrier, which seems totally unassailable to many adults, was crossed with no problem at all by the three-year-olds.

Step 3

Now creativity began to come into play, and the children were asked to suggest items for prayer themselves. Then the leaders would pray about the issues they had raised, and the children would repeat the words after them, as in Step 2. This helped to teach the children that they had to take responsibility for their own prayer.

Step 4

The next step was not only to get the children to suggest issues for prayer, but then for the leaders to suggest *how* they might pray. This might be a set formula into which each of them could slot their own particular people or concerns ('We're going to say in turn a prayer for one of our friends: "Dear Lord Jesus, please look after . . . this week. Amen." Now let's all say it with our friend's name in'). Or if they came up with an ill friend, for example, the leaders might tell them not so much *what* to pray as *how* to: 'You could ask Jesus to give Susie a good night's sleep so that she feels better in the morning.' This is not then too inaccessible for them to put into their own words as a prayer. The leaders can now join heartily in the 'Amen'.

Step 5

Finally they have all the equipment they need to think of an issue, compose a prayer about it and say it out loud. It may have taken them a year and a half to get there, but they've made it, and the goal is reached.

This was the process we used with very young children.

Teaching them at an older age to begin praying out loud is similar in outline, although it is possible to move more quickly through the stages. But along the way I have discovered some additional practical tips. For example, prayers need to be kept short and to the point, and a formula like the one above which can provide a framework for them is helpful at any age. When their turn comes the leaders will need to restrain their verbosity and shorten their prayers into the same formula in order to encourage rather than de-skill the children. The ability of older children to write things down can be a help sometimes: they can write prayers and then read them aloud as a prelude to speaking them straight out of their heads. This should be used sparingly, however, because it is very time consuming, and can feel a bit too much like school. It alienates those who, like my school customers, don't find literacy easy, and it can also breed dependence on pen and paper and thus become counter-productive in birthing extempore prayer.

I worked out this programme to be used with three-year-old children, but since I first went to print with it many people have told me how effective they have found it in adult groups. We used something very like it in the Alpha courses in our church, often with a group of complete outsiders who by the end of the course ten weeks later were relaxed at praying out loud. A similar aim and a similar process are to be found in a small-group course called *Saints at Prayer*.[1]

I have also found ways to deal with two common fears people have when learning to pray aloud: (1) that they'll 'clash' with somebody else who begins their prayer at the same time, and (2) that they won't be able to think of anything to say because someone else has prayed about the sub-

---

[1] M. Mitton, *Saints at Prayer* (Anglican Renewal Ministries, 1994).

ject they had up their sleeve. First, we use an object (often a Bible, although anything at all would do) which is passed round the circle rather like the conch in *Lord of the Flies*, signifying the inalienable right of whoever has it at the time to speak uninterrupted. Once it has gone round once and all have prayed, it can be put in the middle for anyone to pick up if they want to pray further. So far children haven't seemed worried about the possibility of two people grabbing for it at the same time.

The other thing is to teach about the importance of covering a subject in prayer from every angle. Thus if children (or adults, many of whom need to learn this lesson too) were praying for a girl who has gone from the church to work in Africa for a year, they could be encouraged not just to pray 'for Cathryn in Africa, Amen', but to pray in turn for her health, her friendships, the people she'll work with, settling in, getting used to the funny food, her mum and dad who'll miss her, and so on. This creative use of imagination in prayer can draw prayers out of children rather than restricting them because someone else has 'done' Cathryn.

Once they've learned the basics, they can be led further along that journey into prayer which none of us has yet finished. They can be taught to expect answers, and helped to identify them when they come. One resource for this is the 'Prayer Rainbow' which we use with our children's group, rather in the way that some adults use a prayer notebook. A large painted rainbow (which the children enjoyed making) fills the noticeboard, and after our prayer time the gists of some of the prayers are written onto small cards and pinned onto it. The idea is that we can come back at a later stage to look for those things that have been answered, so that we can thank God, and those things that still need our attention, so that we can learn persistence in prayer. There is also the opportunity now and then to teach children about 'un-answered' prayer!

Then they can be taught about different ways of praying. The small steps programme has provided them with the basic skills of prayer, which can then be enhanced by such things as liturgy, written prayers, the use of objects (stones and bits of play dough were used on one occasion to bring to life some prayers around Ezekiel 36), movement and dance as prayer, and so on. We used an enlarged map of the parish on one occasion so that children could stick pins into the appropriate place and pray for their friends and neighbours to become Christians, and we invited children to bring in their school class photos so we could all pray for our friends, and even prayed over a copy of the staff photo from each of the schools in our patch. They also made prayer cards to keep by their beds to encourage them to pray daily for one special person whom they were targeting.[2] Different aspects of prayer can be taught with the use of a mnemonic such as ACTS (Adoration, Confession, Thanksgiving, Supplication), although of course the jargon needs to be unpacked. Maybe you could invent your own mnemonic together.

They can learn too about listening to God in prayer, and ministering in prayer to one another (each the subject of a later chapter). But I believe the basic skills of extempore prayer need to come first. Once a child has been taught to use a pencil and paper, he can then learn to draw, write, scribble, doodle, sketch, design and so on. But without the basics his artistic life will be severely hampered! So it is with the basics of communicating with God.

---

[2] For more ideas on creative prayer, see my *100 Worship Activities for Children* (Kingsway, 2000).

Practice

Once children have learned some of the basics you will need to make sure there are plenty of opportunities for them to put their new-found skills into operation. I have visited churches where we have worked intensively on open prayer. After I left, the leaders, feeling that we had now 'done' that, moved on to something else altogether. Needless to say, the children quickly lost what they had gained, and the whole process had to be repeated, probably with more difficulty, since they had to overcome the 'we tried that and it didn't work' mentality. So for the next few weeks keep on coming back to it; make sure that nothing whatsoever squeezes out your prayer time, until the whole thing is so firmly established that it becomes quite natural.

Integration

The final step is to make sure that praying as a group remains on the agenda – not as it were in its own right, but simply as another tool you might use in other areas. You might move on, for example, to praying for one another in a hands-on way, in what is usually called 'prayer ministry'. The primary emphasis will be on learning how to do this, but the skill gained in extempore prayer will be used in the process.

As well as helping children acquire the basic skills and grow up in their praying, we surely want to do a deeper work still, by instilling in them a love of praying that will stay with them all their lives. The secret is lots of variety and creativity, so that prayer in the group never gets to the point of being a drudge or a bore. Some of us adults who were brought up with, or even live now with, a much more restricted view of what prayer is and how we do it may need to broaden our own horizons in order to feed and excite the children in our care. Drawing, writing, moving, listening, silence, crying: all these activities and many besides can be prayer if done in a Godward direction with the aim of communicating with our Father in heaven.[3]

Is all this a bit 'parental', imposing on children our way of doing things, and manipulating them so they learn to do it? Not if you believe ultimately that being able to pray is going to do them good. As parents John and I have no difficulty whatsoever with making our young daughter clean her teeth each day, and we will use fair means or foul to get it to happen, because we can see around us and have indeed felt at times within our own flesh the consequences of neglect! In the same way, when we look at the sick state of many Christians who have never learned to converse naturally with their Lord, friend and brother, we don't mind how we help the children in our care to avoid such problems.

I can't leave this subject without a look at the area of prayer in tongues. Colin Urquhart, one of the early pioneers of charismatic renewal in Britain in the 1960s and 70s wrote a chapter entitled 'Even our children' in his book about those early days, *When the Spirit Comes*,[4] which tells of the experiences of the children of his church being baptised in the Spirit and receiving the gift of tongues. While 27 years ago this was the most controversial chapter of a controversial book, it is fairly well accepted in charismatic circles nowadays that this gift is available for us and for our children. But we're not

[3] See Richard Foster's excellent *Prayer* (Hodder & Stoughton, 1992) for an account of many different ways of praying.
[4] Colin Urquhart, *When the Spirit Comes* (Hodder & Stoughton, 1974), pp. 59ff.

quite so experienced in knowing how to help children receive it. We won't enter here into any debate about the nature of tongues or the age limits God is thought to have put on it; we'll simply report on our experience of leading children into it.[5]

Vision

The same process applies: our vision is to see the children fluent in the use of this gift. I'm not convinced that you can prove from the Bible that everyone should have this gift, but I am pretty convinced from experience that anyone who wants it can get it eventually, and that children have far less trouble with it than adults. I'll say a bit about my understanding of the nature of the gift later, so as not to disturb the flow now, but I have always worked on the basis that to introduce children to the use of a private prayer language, as well as being a good and scriptural thing in its own right, can also be a gateway into the public use of the gift for the edification of others. Not all will be used in public speaking, but I believe all may receive the gift for private use.

Small steps

The small steps programme for releasing children into tongues is not so much a gradual process through an extended period of time as a breaking down of the immediate task into manageable stages. My methodology is pretty similar in principle to the one I would use with adults, although of course

---

[5] Peter Lawrence, in *Doing What Comes Supernaturally* (Terra Nova, 1997), pp. 106ff has a helpful methodology for ministering to people seeking the gift of tongues. Ours is slightly different but complementary.

children won't have half the hang-ups they do. It's helpful to think of five steps: preparation, explanation, ministry, experimentation and follow-up. An actual session might look something like this.

Preparation

First of all there needs to be some sort of biblical and practical teaching that introduces the whole subject and puts it on the personal agenda of the children. As with the subject of praying, I try to avoid any jargon. I talk about a 'special language' which God gives them to help them talk to him, and leaders demonstrate for them to hear (they do seem to value this experience). But above all we try to help them understand that this is something they can receive, and will find helpful in living for Jesus.

With adults, of course, this part is absolutely crucial. They may be filled with horrific fantasies about how tongues will get out of control, how they'll suddenly start doing it during Evensong, or even worse on the bus to work! They'll also be under the more subtle but equally destructive illusion that it will make them feel wonderfully ecstatic to pray in tongues, or that they'll never need to read their Bibles again once they've got this hotline, or any of the myriad misunderstandings that those who use the gift know to be total nonsense, but about which we all worried before we began.

Children won't have many of these hang-ups at all, unless of course they've been fed them by ignorant adults, but there still needs to be some sort of information about the nature of the gift. This preparation should culminate in an opportunity for a personal response by each child.

Explanation

When it comes to praying for the children, they need at the

outset to know what the actual ministry process will involve:
this is what I'm going to do, this is what God'll do, this is
what you need to do, and this is what should happen.

They'll need to be told, for example, that we would like
them to stand up but stay as relaxed as they can, and that
those praying for them will ask God to send his Holy Spirit
and give them the special language. They shouldn't try to do
the praying themselves, but just think about Jesus. They may
hear the people with them begin to speak in their language,
and they may or may not feel funny, warm, wobbly or whatever. They'll need to be told that it's up to them to do the talking, and that they may need to practise a bit, just as they did
when learning their native language, before they become
really fluent. Above all they need to be reassured that God is
going to do something wonderful for them because he loves
them so much. But keep it all as low-key and matter-of-fact as
you can. If you're in any way nervous or insecure, they'll pick
it up and it will get in the way.

Ministry

When all the explaining has been done you can proceed to
praying for them. The art here is again to keep it as simple
and low-key as you can. As before, this is especially important in adults, who may be so tense that they can't even speak
English, never mind the tongues of angels. Having 17 people
pressing your head down between your shoulders, while
shouting in an incomprehensible language and commanding
you to join in, does not provide the best context to help a terrified person to enter into the fullness of the Lord's blessing.
When ministering to children this is totally unnecessary. A
quick prayer, with a hand laid gently on their head, along the
lines of 'Dear Lord Jesus, please give Joey a special language
to praise you. Amen' is all that's required.

Sometimes even this much is a bit superfluous. On one occasion I was working with a mixed group of adults and children, during which I mentioned in passing the gift of tongues. A girl aged ten interrupted and asked me what 'tongues' was. I didn't want to spoil the flow of what we were doing, so I said I'd talk to her after the session. When we finished she immediately approached me and asked again. I gave a quick explanation of the gift, and then asked if she had ever heard anyone using it. She hadn't, so I asked if she would like to hear me. She said she would, so I demonstrated for a few seconds. 'Wow, that's great!' she said. 'Can I have a go?' I was just about to begin praying for her, when she looked me straight in the eyes and started praising God in tongues! I prayed for her anyway, but it was a prayer of thanks, not of request.

Sometimes it isn't quite as easy as that, although children seem to be very matter-of-fact about it, even if they have to wait a while. A seven-year-old wrote me this note recently:

On Monday I asked Jesus for tounges [sic]. Nothing happened. So I came to the ministry time. Nothing happened. Then on Wednesday I got tounges [sic] when I wasn't expecting it. Love, Katie.

Experimentation

The fourth stage provides an opportunity for them to have a go, and it can be done in two opposite but equally effective ways. The first is for the leader to pray out loud using their language, inviting the child to join in with them, even copying their words if that will help to get them started. The second, which can work either on its own or after a time spent using the first, is to ask the children to go off by themselves somewhere and try out alone what God's given them. They're usually told to find a place where no one else can hear them, and try out loud to say or sing anything that comes into their head, no matter how faltering or how daft. We tend to give them a time limit for this, say five minutes, after which they must report back.

Follow-up

In this final phase, they come back and are asked if they feel God gave them the special language. As a rule, children will say, 'Yes, thank you,' and adults will say, 'Well, I did make a few noises, but I was making it up myself.' Reassure them using Luke 11:13 that as they've asked God for something good, he won't disappoint them, but warn them that before long the Enemy will whisper in their ear that it's just them making up gobbledegook or, even worse, that it's a satanic counterfeit. Tell them it isn't, and that they should tell him to go away. I often make adults promise faithfully that they'll get an egg-timer, and each day for the next week they'll set it for five minutes and make their funny noises, no matter how silly they feel, how strongly the Enemy tells them to stop, however boring it gets, or whatever. I guarantee that by the end of the week they'll be reasonably fluent, and I've not had many dissatisfied customers yet.

There are some people (only ever adults, in my experience) who simply cannot get it to happen for them. Probably the least helpful thing to do is to pray again, only a bit harder. We usually encourage people to leave it, and not to let the whole thing become a big overriding issue. They can have another go later. In the meantime they are no less important and valuable to God, with or without tongues. But if we can get our children confident in the gift while they are still young and innocent of hang-ups, so much the better – we could be saving lots of frustration later on.

Practice

The children will of course then need instruction in the use of the gift, and there are plenty of good books on this subject, which, although aimed at adults, can be useful resources for the leaders in taking the children forward.[6] They will also need opportunities to put into use the gift they have received, and appropriate space should be built into the programme and activities for this. We have found sessions of singing in the Spirit during worship times with the children to be helpful.

Leaders will need sensitivity in deciding how to deal with the parents of children who have received the gift: there is a tension between confidentiality and the need for sympathetic nurture of the children. Ideally the children should be encouraged to tell their parents about the experience at the earliest opportunity, but leaders ought to have some kind of awareness of the range of likely responses. There will be those parents who are overjoyed, those who believe the gifts died out at the end of the apostolic age, and those who are not Christians at all and think we've done something weird and sinister to their offspring. I'll have more to say on the delicate relationship with parents in Chapter 11.

Integration

As with extempore prayer, discussed above, the time will come when the focus moves away from the gift of tongues

---

[6] I have found among the most helpful: D. & R. Bennett, *The Holy Spirit and You* (Kingsway, 1971), pp. 93ff (30 years old and American, but still a classic); D. Pytches, *Come Holy Spirit* (Hodder & Stoughton, 1985), pp. 62ff (a good guide from the Vineyard point of view) and D. Watson, *Discipleship* (Hodder & Stoughton, 1981), pp. 95ff.

because it has become firmly established simply as something we do. The gift can be spoken about and used quite naturally, and will remain in the group's prayer repertoire, even though it may not be a major issue every week.

The final thing I would say here (because I've never seen it clearly taught anywhere else) is that I believe there are in fact not one but two gifts of tongues: *public* and *private*. The public gift is to be spoken out under the direct inspiration of the Spirit during a meeting or service, and it should be interpreted for the benefit of others. The private gift, on the other hand, is the only gift that is the possession of the speaker, who can turn it on and off at will, rather than waiting for the inspiration of the Spirit. It is for private use rather than public consumption. Once you understand this, it makes sense of the seemingly ambivalent material in 1 Corinthians 12–14 where Paul is apparently unable to make up his mind whether he likes the gift or not, and it makes clear the different uses the different gifts have. Paul wants us all to speak in private tongues (14:5), but not everyone does so publicly (12:30); rather only two or three should speak out publicly in a service (14:27). He thinks they would do well to lay off public tongues a bit and concentrate instead on the higher gifts like prophecy (14:5), yet he thanks God that he does it (presumably privately) more than any of them (14:18). The problem in Corinth was that private tongues was being used publicly, and a correct understanding of the difference can avoid excess on the one hand, but also encourage increase in the gift on the other. Children needn't be aware of all this controversy; they can just learn from the experience of the generation that pioneered renewal in the twentieth century and get it right from the start.

> Prayer is the simplest form of speech
> That infant lips can try;
> Prayer, the sublimest strains that reach
> The Majesty on high.

The words of James Montgomery's hymn emphasise the simplicity and yet the supreme importance of prayer in the life of the Christian disciple. Sadly many of us live with crippled prayer lives. The more we can do to save future generations from this fate by training them into good habits early, the better for them and for the kingdom of God.

6

Hearing God

Once children are relaxed and competent at speaking to God, the next step is to move them into hearing him speak back. This leads us into the whole area of the prophetic, and before we begin to think about how to help children into it, I'd better define briefly what I mean by 'prophetic', since children's leaders will need to think through this complex area if they are to deal with it helpfully and accessibly.

The gift of prophecy is one that Paul talks about at length in 1 Corinthians 12–14. He seems quite keen on it, and tells his friends that they should seek it earnestly (1 Corinthians 14:1). But what is it? Well, it depends whom you ask.

In the early days of charismatic renewal in this country, it was easy to spot prophecy: someone stood up in church with their heart palpitating and their hair on end and said, 'My children, I love you,' or something similar. Prophecy as manifested in the local church was often (although not exclusively) fairly low-key, but at times very powerful and edifying for all that. But there were other bits of the church that seemed to be in at a completely different level. When they sought to prophesy, it was for the nation, not just a home group, and they seemed very interested in what was happening in Israel. They would spend time up mountains, and would return with revelations of world-shattering significance, even if few in the world ever got to hear about them.

And then, of course, there were the Kansas City Prophets, perhaps the most controversial prophetic movement of all in recent years. Their relationship with John Wimber gave them a ready platform in England, and you loved them or hated them (some of the other prophets hated them, or rather their approach to prophecy). A self-respecting prophet in the Kansas City tradition would prophesy about earthquakes, droughts and such like, and would seek individual prophecies that laid bare the secrets of a person's heart.[1]

Along with this came some discussion about 'When is a prophet not a prophet?' The increased popularity of 'words of knowledge' has led some to ask about whether the dividing line between the different spiritual gifts in 1 Corinthians 12 is as clear as we were taught in the 1960s and 70s.

I mention all this because each of these different controversies has in its own way had the effect of de-skilling the church every bit as much as it has of enabling us – maybe even more so. No doubt there have been tremendous benefits from these different schools, and I myself have valued my exposure to most of them, but at the same time it can all seem a bit beyond mere mortals like us, and indeed like our children. If we are to lead children into prophetic gifts (and the whole thrust of this book is that we should), we must know what we

---

[1] A good and sympathetic account of the Kansas City Prophets, their relationship with John Wimber, and the controversy they stirred up, is given in David Pytches, *Some Said It Thundered* (Hodder & Stoughton, 1990). Others, less sympathetic, have renamed this book 'Some Said They Blundered'.

understand ourselves to be leading them into, and we must have confidence that they can be led there. A requirement of earthquakes may not help us to be very confident!

My approach of late has been to be very much more low-key about the whole thing. For a start I talk about 'the prophetic', 'prophetic gifts' or even, with John Wimber, 'revelatory gifts'. This moves us away from the idea of a specific 'gift of prophecy' which is not the same as a 'word of knowledge', a 'vision' or what have you. Instead I see a continuum by which God reveals information to us, which may be a long speech, a simple bit of knowledge, a picture, a series of moving pictures, or even just a vague impression or feeling. Was something a proper 'prophecy' or not? Who knows? It just told us something that God wanted to say. Seeing revelatory gifts in this way means that quite a few people who would never call themselves 'prophets' do in fact move regularly in this area. This approach neither denies nor denigrates the ministry of those who clearly are 'prophets', moving in much greater revelatory power; it just allows us to begin where we are.

Next, my observation of and involvement in the phenomenon known as 'prophetic worship'[2] has made me question the understanding of prophecy as something that comes exclusively 'down' from God to us. Songs or music given spontaneously may contain what God wants to say to us, but may equally be expressions of what the Spirit living in our own hearts wants to say to our Father God. Mary's prophetic outpouring known as the Magnificat (Luke 1:48–55) surely

[2] For details of this see J. King, *Leading Worship* (Kingsway, 1988), pp. 114ff, or D. Fellingham, *Worship Restored* (Kingsway, 1987), pp. 40ff. Both are now out of print although the latter is included in *Classics on Worship* (Kingsway, 1999).

comes into this category. And even this may not be that hard-and-fast: one prophetic expression may contain both 'upwards' and 'downwards' elements. So all in all I try to be pretty all-inclusive about what the prophetic actually is.

There are two things to take into account before we begin. The first is that to get prophecy firmly established in a church or a children's group takes time. When they were younger our boys enjoyed jigsaw puzzles, and as far as they were concerned the more pieces the better. We often had one on the go, on a table on the landing where it wouldn't have to be cleared up every meal time. This they referred to as their 'big-term project', and it could take months to complete, a few pieces at a time. Prophecy, and also, incidentally, nearly everything else we'll need to teach children, is a 'big-term project'. One of the most common mistakes among enthusiastic children's workers is to lose focus and try to make sure they get over everything they know about the subject in question in one session. Children simply don't learn that way (and neither, we suspect, do adults). So each session might be simply about putting a few pieces in place, so that they join on to the bits already there. The picture isn't finished, but it's beginning to take shape. Maybe an aim for a single jigsaw session might be just to finish that lady's face, or fill in the elephant's left ear, or whatever. So with the prophetic: learning is a process, and it'll take time. You can't spend a week on it and feel you've 'done' prophecy now. Hence the need for a similar kind of small steps programme to those we've already discussed.

The second thing to understand is that there is one significant difference between the prophetic and the other major spiritual gift we mentioned in the last chapter, tongues. An important thing to realise about tongues, and a thing which cuts both ways, is that it's pretty black and white. Apart from a brief learning stage (usually no longer than days) you can either do it or you can't. You've either done it before or you haven't, and you've generally noticed if you have. Therefore leading children into the manifestation of this gift is like making a new start. It's a breakthrough, a whole new experience, a quantum leap from where they were before. Prophetic gifts are different. The chances are that many children have already experienced something of it without knowing. This may have been anything from a vague sense of God in their minds to a full-blown word of knowledge.

My daughter Vicki was walking with me up the long side driveway to our house one winter evening in the dark. Suddenly she squeezed my hand and said, 'Don't worry, God is looking after me.'

'Who told you that?' I asked.

'God did,' came the matter-of-fact reply. This happened some months before her second birthday.

One four-year-old in a previous church went up to a lady in the congregation and announced confidently, 'There are *two* babies in your tummy!' The woman had in fact just discovered a few days previously that she was pregnant, and sure enough gave birth to twins in due course. The little girl had had no direct teaching on prophecy that we knew about, apart from being brought up by Spirit-filled parents, but it would have been a nonsense to begin teaching her as if she'd never had anything to do with the prophetic. Small children do quite often hear God, so instructing them in prophecy is much more about naming and refining a phenomenon than introducing it.

So with that important background, how might we go about leading children on in this area? The same four-stage process of vision, small steps, practice and integration can be helpful here, although with some refinements particular to the nature of this gift.

Vision

Where do you see this going long term? My vision was to train up a group of children to be able to hear God's voice, to learn how it might most commonly come to each of them, and to be able to test and discern what was God and what wasn't. I wanted to see children confident in speaking out God's heart should he speak at any time during a session or at other times, and yet aware that they might well have got it partially or even totally wrong, so that they offered what they thought they had heard humbly. If they hadn't got it right, they would know that they were still loved and accepted, and that it was OK to get things wrong. So how do we get to there from here?

Small steps

I found it most helpful to break this journey down into five small steps, followed by three sub-headings in the 'practice' section.

Teaching

Many people who, like me, were brought up as evangelical Christians were often told that prayer was a two-way thing, and that they should listen to God as well as speak to him. But few of us were ever given any idea about how this might happen, other than the possibility of Bible verses jumping out and hitting us. It is curious that with such a high degree of emphasis placed on the Bible, we failed to notice the sheer variety of ways in which God spoke to people in Bible times. Visions, dreams, angels, trances, audible voices and even on one occasion a donkey's voice: all these were used by God to speak to his people. So why the limit? Teaching on God speaking, and the ways in which we might hear him, needs to be built into the curriculum of the children's ministry, and it needs to be backed up with workshop-style sessions where the children can begin to experience for themselves what they're learning about. We'll return to the importance of God's written word in the Bible later, but we shouldn't limit children to only one way of hearing him.

Part of the teaching task, as I have mentioned, is the affirmation of children's previous experiences of hearing God. These may be gently explored and recognised, and will provide a very helpful way in for those for whom such experiences have been common, but who have never understood the nature of them.

Preparing

Teaching provides a general background, and puts the subject on the agenda, but before beginning to move into the prophetic some more specific work needs to be done. As with tongues, children need to be told what might happen, and what they have to do themselves. We teach them that revelation might come in one of five ways (ways we learned from John Wimber's ministry): you see it (a mental picture), you hear it (in your mind or even audibly), you feel it (a sensation or pain in a particular part of your own body which may help identify a need for healing in someone else, or sometimes a sense of what God feels about a particular situation), you know it (just an overwhelming certainty about something), or you say it (it comes out of your mouth before your brain has had time to intervene and tell you you're making it up). Most of the children I've worked with over the years would be able to tell you this, because it has been drummed into them over a period of time, and also because they would have experienced some of them for themselves. Children need to understand as well that while God gives the prophecy, they are the prophets.

Rarely is it like reading a script that God has inspired verbatim: most of the time an idea or impression needs to be clothed in words or drawn out by a human being, who will put the stamp of their own personality on it. Children may have heard adults who were brought up on the Authorised Version of the Bible prophesying in that kind of language, and that is fine for them, but it needs to be explained that there is no need to imitate the rather 'Old Testament' style for a prophecy to be genuine. They can clothe it in words appropriate for their culture. It is probably true that this mixture of human and divine means that a pure one hundred degree proof prophecy is a very rare if not non-existent thing. Most of the time there will be a mixture of what is from God and what is from us (and it will not necessarily be bad for that).

Children can be told to expect a sketchy revelation ('a snapshot' is more accessible terminology for them than 'a vision') but that they can often get more by taking what they have received back to God and asking for further details. On one occasion our children's group was learning about words of knowledge, and were then going on to experiment. I prayed for God's Spirit to come and speak to the children, and almost before I'd finished two children spoke up, one with a sense of someone with a hurt wrist, and the other with a picture of a house on fire. These were shared with the group, but no one seemed interested in responding. So the two 'prophets' were invited to ask God for more details. After a short while the 'wrist' person said that the wrist in question had been hurt during PE at school last Friday, and the 'house' person knew that it wasn't an actual house on fire, but that someone was frightened about the possibility of their house catching fire. Immediately there was a response: someone had in fact hurt their wrist in PE on Friday, and they then received prayer for healing; and someone else had spent the night in his parents' bed after a particularly disturbing dream during which his house had caught fire. He too was prayed for to break the grip of the lingering fear. Much of the time when our words don't seem to mean anything, it may be because we haven't taken this vital step of asking God for more.

As well as preparing children for what God may do, we also prepare them for what the Enemy almost certainly will do. I usually explain to them how much he doesn't want God's words spoken to us, since they are always to do us good and he only wants to do us harm, so he tells us every time God speaks that we are only making it up, and we'll feel silly if we tell people out loud. I train them to respond to the Enemy in the only way he deserves: by ignoring him and getting on with it anyway! They learn this lesson quickly when they see events like those described above taking place, and realise how much the Enemy would rob us of God's blessing if we let him.

Modelling

The third step, which is not really a step at all but should run concurrently with the first two, is that children should see the prophetic modelled. If yours is a switched-on sort of church where prophecy is a regular part of what goes on each Sunday, there won't be a problem here, but if your children are in fact way ahead of the adults, or if most of the serious adult spirituality takes place once the children are safely out of the way in their own groups, they may never have seen the prophetic working in a church service or group. This is where the children's leadership is important: they should be confident in moving in the prophetic, so that the children can see it as well as learn about it.

Listening

After all the explaining has been done, children need an opportunity to practise it for themselves. Most commonly I would use worship as a context for hearing God, not just because we're often more tuned in when we worship, but also because I take seriously a theology which says that God is more manifestly present with us when we worship him. To those who would say that this is manipulative emotionalism, I would say first of all that it is scriptural (see 2 Kings 3:15 where Elisha struck up on his harp to attune himself with God's heart), and second that the practice of hearing God in the context of worship enables us to practise and master the art of hearing him elsewhere.

So at the end of a worship time, we would ask God to come and speak to us. This might be very general, or it might be more directed. Sometimes the leaders will simply ask if anyone sees, hears, feels, knows or wants to say anything, while on other occasions there may be a more specific target. Our children were doing a series on sharing their faith, and had talked about the need for constant targeted prayer. They had made and coloured little cards something like this:

Dear God, thank you that you love _____.
Please help [him/her] to get to know you as a friend.
Please help me to share you with [him/her]. Amen.

The idea was that this was kept by their beds as a daily reminder to pray, perhaps with a photo or picture of their chosen friend on it. All that was required was for God to fill in the blank, so the children prayed and asked God to show them the one person he wanted this special prayer effort to go on. On other occasions healing may be on the agenda, so we

might ask God to give specific words of knowledge like those
mentioned above.

Other things can be used to encourage children to hear
God. They can be put into small groups and asked, 'If God
were here, what might he want to say to each of the other
members of your foursome?' Not only does this encourage
them to listen, but it also introduces them to the idea that God
may give personal words for specific people. Physical objects
can be helpful as we listen to God. On one occasion we used
stones and play dough to help us understand God's desire to
give us new and soft hearts. During a listening time after this
exercise one little boy said that God had shown him how hor-
rible he often was to his brother, and how it upset both his
brother and God. There was prayer and ministry for forgiveness, and it subsequently proved to be a significant turning
point in the life of that family.

On another occasion I had been playing with a large group
of younger children with a parachute. I'd taught them previously how to hear God ('You see it, you hear it, you feel it,
you know it, you say it'), so they stopped parachuting and
prayed for a moment for God to speak to them about himself
through what they were doing. The range of things the children heard was amazing: from colour and joy to being
wrapped up in God's love; being protected by him. One child
even saw in the red panels a picture of Jesus' blood flowing
down from the cross onto him to wash him clean. In the Bible
everyday objects (the concordance doesn't mention para-
chutes, but pots get quite a good look in) are often the means
of God's revelation, and they are a real gift to us when we
work with young children.

Telling

Having given the opportunity for God to speak, the final small step is to give the opportunity for the children to tell others what they've heard. One important factor to remember here is that children, especially young ones, will not usually think (or hear God) in words, but in pictures. So it is helpful to have some pencils and paper handy for them to draw what it is they've seen in their minds. The older and more articulate among them may be able to use language to describe their revelations, but a picture-based sharing of what God has said is often more useful. It may also be helpful to tell a small sub-group before talking to the whole group, especially if it is a large one. To tell a few friends, with a trusted leader, feels much safer. The skilful leader can then tell the rest of the group in a way that draws the child out a bit: 'It was a *big* house you saw, wasn't it, Sally?' Sally can then begin to fill in details in the presence of the whole group, which will build her confidence for next time.

These small steps may happen quite quickly, or they may take a few weeks if there is a considerable amount of background teaching to cover. However, it is quite important actually to do something before too long rather than just talk about it. If there is any fear-driven procrastination going on among the leaders, the children will very quickly detect it and become infected with nervousness themselves.

Once you have got the children to the point of hearing God reasonably easily, you will need to practise for a few weeks. However, in this particular instance practising doesn't simply mean doing lots more of the same. There are three areas in particular where there will need to be growth in understanding and technique.

Practice

Testing

The Bible is very clear that anything claiming to be a so-
called prophetic revelation should be tested, and I would want
to emphasise strongly that children should be taught the
importance of this. As a clergy wife I am only too well aware
of the havoc that can be wrought in churches by 'prophets'
who feel they are above correction or discernment (they often
feel they're above the leadership of the church too!). I have no
desire to add to the revelation God has given us once and for
all in the Bible, and I have always taught children to value
Scripture and to look to it as their final authority. But having
said that, I would want to do all I can to be encouraging. To
stand up publicly and denounce a child's first faltering
attempts at sharing what they feel God has said to them as
'false prophecy' may put them off for life. My aim, if I possibly can do so, is to endorse whatever it is they say and to con-
gratulate them for it. There are times when correction is needed: when one little girl told us that God had said she needn't
eat jam sandwiches if she didn't want to, we quickly discerned a domestic dispute over which she wanted divine
backing! On another occasion a child felt that he had heard
God saying that absolutely everyone was going to end up in
heaven. This too needed correcting, this time from a doctrinal
point of view. Even situations like these, though, can be
turned into valuable teaching opportunities in the hands of an
encouraging but creative leader.

The basic understanding here is that it is more important to
encourage the prophet than to get the prophecy word perfect.
A relaxed attitude will give children encouragement to try
again, and the teaching they receive each week will be training them more and more to know God's heart and understand

the kind of things he's likely to be saying. If they do get it wrong it's rarely malicious; it's just that they don't yet know him very well and therefore haven't learned to filter out the bits that are much more from them than from him. They need helping with this, not slapping down and 'correcting' in a way that will stop them ever trying again.

Responding

An important and quite liberating insight which came from John Wimber's teaching on the prophetic is the difference between revelation, interpretation and application. In a nutshell it means that to be a prophet is a bit like being a postman. When ours delivers the gas bill (which he seems to do with alarming frequency) he has got into the habit of simply sticking it through the letter box and going away again. We would be quite put out if he were to knock at the door, tell us how many units we'd used and why, and insist that we stop what we're doing, go into town there and then, get some money out of the building society, and pay it. His job is to deliver the message and let us decide what to do from there on. When (occasionally) we bury it under a heap of other papers and forget about it, and a nasty red letter from the gas company arrives, that simply is nothing to do with the postman. It's our problem, not his.

If only some 'prophets' could learn this lesson! There is a common feeling that a hotline to God is the sole preserve of those with prophetic gifts, and an equally common set of disaster stories about what happens when the prophets try to take over the running of a church, writing off the leadership for the dullness of their spiritual ears (in other words they won't do what we say God has told them to). The job of the prophet is to hear God; they or others or the church as a whole need to discern the interpretation of that revelation, and the leadership

needs to decide how, if at all, the word is to be applied and
what action needs to be taken. If a church dramatically
ignores something God has said, and misses some golden
opportunity or other, the prophet will one day have to stand
before God to be asked, 'Did you deliver my message?' If he
or she did, that is all God requires. It is the church leaders
who will be asked, 'Why didn't you do something about what
I told you?'

So children need to be taught early on that when they hear
from God they offer it, and leave the rest to others. It may
even be that they need to keep it and offer it to someone else
at a later stage, although they won't be very good at this when
they're young. Obviously with their 'encouraging' brief, the
leaders will do all they can to find *something* about the word
or picture to respond to, but children need to feel they've dis-
charged their responsibility fully if they've just told someone.
They don't even need to understand what they've said – only
that someone else will, and that's up to God now.

Constant feedback is important so that the children can hear
what has gone on during the week. My experience is that
people don't always respond there and then to words of
knowledge or prophecies, but will often come back later and
say something like, 'I didn't like to say at the time, but that
picture was just right for me.' This is infuriating, if under-
standable, but needn't rob us of the joy of having got something right if we make sure we do report back regularly. When
the church of which John was Vicar first began to move into
words of knowledge we kept a careful note of words given
and words responded to. We found over a period of about a
year that we had something like a 75 per cent success rate, but
that only about 10 per cent of the words were claimed at the
same time or in the same service as they were given. Without
this feedback we could have become very discouraged, and so

can our children if they think that their so-called revelations are constantly meaningless.

They also need to learn, however, that they don't have a divine right to having their prophecies acted upon. That's up to the leaders. It may not be the case in the early stages that God will reveal his life-changing purposes for the church through the children (although of course he might), but to teach them these principles from the start will lay good foundations for the church of the future.

Refining

If prophecies need to be tested, prophets need to be refined. God may choose to give important messages through immature people, but they don't have to stay immature. This is true of all ages, but particularly so with children. The problem with them is that they're so young! One minute they may be rapt in worship or giving a profound word from the Lord, but the next they'll be mucking about, pinching the little girl next to them and making rude noises with their bottoms. I heard one church leader telling about a service where some of the teenagers, lined up at the back of the church, had brought with them some Blu-tak, and spent most of the worship time modelling different shaped noses for themselves and each other, which of course they found tremendously amusing. The leader caught the eye of one of them with a piercing glare, and he immediately joined in the worship. This young person came forward a few minutes later to give a prophetic word that was formative in setting the whole direction of the children's ministry in that church for the next couple of years.

Because there is a tendency for most adults to feel that spiritual gifts, and perhaps especially prophecy, are for saints of the higher degrees only, they can easily feel one of two things: that children who aspire to such things are saints of the higher

degrees, or, that since their behaviour shows clearly that they
are not, the 'prophecies' simply can't be genuine. In fact the
truth is that they are just kids, and while God may gift them
supernaturally from time to time, he seldom makes them grow
up supernaturally, usually preferring to let nature and good
parenting take its course. Thus in children we have a paradox:
profound reverence and a model for spirituality that Jesus said
adults should emulate, mixed up with mischief, immaturity
and silliness, with the two succeeding each other by minutes
or even seconds. The onus is again on the leaders to work at
the big-term project of discipleship, while neither despising
the children's attempts to hear God, nor expecting them to be
old before their time.

And when you come to think of it, is it all that different
with adults? How many people get up from kneeling at the
communion rail in our churches, having received as the cli-
max to their worship the bread and wine which speak of
Christ's undying love, and the living sacrifices we offer to
him, only to be whispering to their neighbour a few moments
later, 'Look at her hat! What does she look like? And have
you heard about her daughter and the electric man? Well . . .'?
Maybe the only difference is that children aren't so clever at
being naughty quietly.

Integration

As I've explained earlier, the 'integration' phase is simply
about making sure that once your emphasis moves away from
prophecy and onto your next big-term project, there are still
opportunities from time to time to listen to God and expect to
hear him speak. I've mentioned the exercise of asking God to
identify a friend for whom he is calling us specially to pray;
we have used similar times of listening to allow the Holy

Spirit to pinpoint specific sins, potential idols, people to whom we might write encouraging letters and so on. It gets to the stage where it's no big deal. God is present with us, and is quite likely to have something he wants to say.

There is, however, another area of integration that is very much more of a big deal, and although I mention it here in this context, it is as much an issue in the context of other spiritual gifts. I mean the integration of children's spirituality into the life of the whole church. It is one thing for children to be confident enough to share what they think God has said in a safe group, but quite another to do so when the whole congregation is gathered. There might be several hundred people present, and the prospect, and indeed the mechanics, of giving a word of prophecy, may be overwhelmingly daunting. This isn't primarily a book about the use of spiritual gifts in the church, but it might well be worth the while of your leadership to give some thought to ways in which children can be allowed to contribute as the Spirit speaks to them. And in the meantime, keep at it in your groups – you all need as much practice as you can get!

7

Doing the Works of God

Paul was toddling happily around the kitchen while I was at the sink, when there was a sudden cry of pain. I spun round to see Paul sitting on the floor with blood gushing from his hand and tears streaming down his face. Scooping him up, I tried to comfort him and find out what had happened (I never did) and then ran the tap and put his hand under it. There was a large cut on one finger, and although I have no medical qualifications apart from a morbid addiction to *Casualty* on a Saturday evening, I knew that this was going to need stitching. So immediately I pressed my finger on his to stop the flow of blood, shouted for Steve and knelt down on the kitchen floor to pray. Steve (then aged about three or four) said something like, 'Dear Lord Jesus, please make Paul's finger better. Amen.' I let go, to find that the bleeding had stopped completely, and when I ran the tap again to clean it up, I was totally unable to find where the cut had been; there wasn't a mark.

When it comes to healing and the miraculous, children don't have nearly as many hang-ups as adults do, so we need to be very careful as we explore this subject that we don't train children into our doubts. Adult hang-ups have caused

Christians to have so many different views about and approaches to healing that the whole thing can be a bit like a minefield which we tiptoe through nervously while our children skip around in uncaring abandon, never seeming to get blown up at all. Perhaps their lighter weight makes it easier for them, but those of us who are a bit more theologically obese can easily come to grief.

One Sunday a five-year-old girl came to church with cotton wool in her ear because she had an earache. During the service a word of knowledge was shared about someone present with earache, and the girl responded and went for prayer. Later in the day her mum asked her how her ear was now. She was mystified. 'It's all right of course. John prayed for it!' came the indignant reply. Why on earth should we even need to ask? God's done what he said he'd do. Life's like that when you're five!

This same confidence comes over in these feedback notes I received from two seven-year-olds.

One day at scool my friend Liam had exma [sic] and when it was the end of the day I prayed for him and the next day he told me his exma was gone.

When I was on hoilday My Daddys hands were very porly and I praid for them and they got better straigh away.

To children the whole thing is all very matter-of-fact.

In this chapter I simply want to spell out some of the things I've done to lead children into this area, and why I've done it that way, without getting too deeply into arguments about the validity of healing. After that you'll find a continuation of the subject in the next chapter, which is a kind of rag-bag containing some of the less positive and attractive aspects of healing.

First of all, I work with a particular model because it is one I have found to be most accessible for adults and children alike. When we were in parish ministry we found it accessible to adults originally, and it was only as we began to move into this area with children that we realised just how helpful it was to them too. This model is the one taught by the Vineyard movement. It is charismatic and Spirit-led, it has biblical-sized high expectations but also a satisfying theology of failure, and any three-year-old can do it. One of John Wimber's greatest gifts was the ability to analyse and teach what we have already referred to as 'small steps programmes', and his five-stage pattern for the healing ministry is one we have easily adapted for use among children.[1] So what might we actually do in our small steps programme?

Identification

For whom do we pray? Sometimes, as we've already mentioned, the need for prayer may be identified through information that comes out of a time of listening to God. At other times a problem may come to light through discussion, or a request for prayer. Sometimes the leaders can simply ask if anyone has something for which they'd like prayer. Any of these may come from a look at a healing miracle in the Bible – the stories are great faith-builders. If ministry is built into the normal programme, and particularly if children are used to seeing adults ministering to one another in church, it soon becomes a part of the culture, and holds no embarrassment. Children are also gloriously free from the pride that causes

---

[1] For definitive accounts of John Wimber's healing methodology, see his *Power Healing* (Hodder & Stoughton, 1986) and David Pytches, *Come Holy Spirit* (Hodder & Stoughton, 1985).

adults to struggle on without admitting or opening up their need for prayer, and will be only too glad to be on the receiving end of ministry.

As with adults, the nature of the need may vary, and leaders need to grow among their children an understanding that any kind of problem is fair game for the power of the Spirit, and we're just as happy to pray for veruccas as for their argument with Tracey at school or their violin exam the next day. This doesn't cheapen a serious and reverent ministry, as some would suggest; it models a God who cares about every area of their life and who can make a difference in any of them.

Explanation

Having found who it is you're going to pray with, there is once again the need for some kind of explanation of what is about to happen. As usual picture language is most helpful for children. 'You've asked Jesus for something,' we might say, 'and now we're going to ask him as well. So you need to be very quiet for a while, close your eyes, stand still and hold out your hands so that Jesus can give you what we're asking for. You don't need to do any more praying – we'll do that bit; you just concentrate on thinking about Jesus and what he's going to put into your hands.' (We often encourage adults, too, over this last point, by reminding them that if they were having an operation they wouldn't be helping, so they can safely leave the praying to us.)

The other children also need some explanation about their part. We tell them first of all to pray with their eyes open, because they will be able to see what God is doing. I have often used a model which Captain Alan Price of the Teknon Trust, well known for his work with children in the power of the Holy Spirit, calls 'drainpiping'. We tell the children to stand in a group around the person for whom we're praying, and put one hand gently on him, without pressing or hurting him. We then encourage them to lift their other hand in the air towards Father God since it is his power which will release healing to our person and nothing we can do in our own strength. In this way the children are making a picture with their bodies and are being like drainpipes or channels through which the Holy Spirit may flow to others. Captain Alan's experience is that this physical action can help to focus the children's attention for surprisingly longer periods than might usually be expected of them.

Invitation

We then encourage one of them to pray a short prayer: 'Come, Holy Spirit.' This invitation or calling down of the Spirit is a hallmark of Vineyard-style ministry, and this is discussed at some length in *Living Liturgy*.[2] It's not that God isn't there all the time; it's that sometimes his presence is more manifest – he's not just around, but he's actually doing something and we know it, and can feel and see it. It's this kind of powerful presence we seek as we begin to minister to one another. We teach the children how to see the presence of God, and we teach them to wait quietly until they can see it. So, for example, they may see physical changes such as breathing deepening, eyelids fluttering, swaying, shaking or trembling, a facial relaxation or glow, or even 'resting in the Spirit' as they fall to the floor under God's power.

It is important to get over our natural adult reaction to these manifestations as 'weird' and teach children to expect to see them as marks of the Spirit's presence, and to welcome them.

---

[2] John Leach, *Living Liturgy* (Kingsway, 1997), pp. 11ff.

If there is any sense of fear initially, the chances are they'll
have caught it from the adults, but a quick interview afterwards with the person you've prayed for will reassure them
that all was well. I've often asked children to feed back to me
after ministry how they felt. Comments have included: 'I felt
Jesus touch me – it was very soft. I felt safe', 'I felt warm all
over', 'I had a tickly feeling' and 'I saw confetti coming
down on me'. One girl aged six, who had begun a conference
week very negatively, seeking attention, always trying to
escape to the toilet, and disrupting the other children in her
group, finally responded to the Holy Spirit. After ministry she
said she felt peaceful and happy inside. She certainly looked a
lot happier on the outside and was much more co-operative
within the group, joining in happily with the others.

As children grow in this ministry they can be taught a bit
more about what different sorts of physical manifestations
might mean, but they do need to know that it will achieve
very little to begin praying before there is clear evidence that
God has shown up.

Prayer

With adults this bit can go on for hours, but with children it
needs to be short and sweet. Those ministering can be encouraged simply to ask God to do what it is they're after, or to
address the condition and tell it to go, or the bit of the body
telling it to be healed in the name of Jesus. The leader may
ask who'd like to pray, or may ask one of the children,
'Would you like to?' (meaning 'Will you, please?'). The other
children can be encouraged to pray quietly, in their special
prayer language if Jesus has given them one. The leaders need
to find the right balance between modelling the ministry,
encouraging the children into it and stepping back and letting

them get on with it. There is always the temptation to do everything for them, but that will prevent growth rather than facilitate it.

As with the more ordinary prayer we discussed in Chapter 5, it can be helpful to teach children set phrases to use when praying. So to 'break the power of' fear or oppression; to 'command' bits of the body to be healed, or to move back into place; to 'set free' the victim from their illness, to 'cut them off' from unhelpful family ties: all these phrases can be taught in their appropriate context, while of course never neglecting to teach that it is the power of God that heals and not our words. Children must be taught that healing is first and foremost about listening to God, which hopefully they have already learned to do. But having particular phrases in their vocabulary helps them to select something appropriate when God has spoken to them.

As specific prayer begins, there may be more physical manifestations or there may not, but there is almost always some sense of power having been moved around (difficult to explain, but very real to experience). There may also be some periods of silence. Surprisingly children are quite good at this bit because they don't seem to suffer from the temptation to talk God into doing what they want him to do by listing all the reasons why this is a particularly meritorious case and deserving of his attention. They seem to be perfectly happy with 'Dear Jesus, please make Ben's sore throat better. Amen', or 'We tell this poor arm to get better', which is a coincidence because that's just how Jesus seemed to pray when he was ministering healing.

Feedback

Another characteristic of this approach is the desire to know how we've done. It isn't enough just to pray and then move on. We need to talk to the person, ask if they felt anything, if the pain is better, if Jesus showed them anything or spoke to them, or whatever. Children are almost always encouraging, in our experience, and will have felt God touch them in a very welcome and positive way, even if full and complete healing has yet to be seen. Jesus is frequently very powerfully present, and his presence is discerned in tangible ways. Adults will commonly tell you that as a result of your ministry they feel much more peaceful; children are far more likely to have seen Jesus holding them or walking into the difficult situation ahead of them, or whatever. It may be that you can go round a few times with more prayer and more talking about what has or hasn't happened, although our experience is that this is less helpful (and indeed less necessary) with children.

And finally don't forget the longer-term feedback. Testimony is important in building faith and encouraging more prayer and ministry for others, as well as for proving to children that God is alive and well and living in them.

So that's the process, and it takes ten minutes at the most. It's easy to learn and accessible to try out, and I hope you'll find it something you can begin to do yourself if you don't already. But be aware, too, that like all models it isn't the only way to do things, and God might just lead your children to minister in some completely different ways. A friend of mine had been suffering for some months from an infection deep inside one of her ears, which resulted in continual pain and itching. Several different attempts at medication had failed to solve the problem. One morning a two-year-old child was sitting on her lap, fiddling with her hair. Lifting it up, she discovered an ear hiding beneath it, gave the ear a kiss and said, 'There – it's all better now!' My friend thought absolutely nothing of this event until a couple of days later during a church service when she suddenly realised that the pain and irritation had completely gone. She has had no further trouble, and is convinced that God used the child's kiss to minister healing. This is a great story, but I still tend not to teach people when ministering to kiss the affected parts of their patients!

As in the previous chapters you'll need to work hard at a fully integrated healing ministry, beginning with your vision and adding to the small steps plenty of practice until prayer ministry becomes a natural part of what you do week by week.

That, however, is the easy part, and I do need to say a bit more about helping children to move on in healing, both practically and theologically. Three areas particularly demand our attention: growing, first of all, and then in the next chapter failure and a quick word about deliverance and the demonic.

Growing

Quite a few books have been written that very helpfully lead adults further on in the healing ministry, and I've given details of some of them in the footnotes. It ought to be possible to write a children's version of them, but a more helpful way would be for leaders to be able to immerse themselves in the theory and practice of the healing ministry, and then use their understanding of children to translate it all to their level, and to teach it at their level. This is, after all, how teachers are trained: I spent four years at college, and my estimate is that 70 per cent of the time was spent on history and only 30 per cent on learning about children and education. That's why children's work must never be seen as the soft option in the church. Leaders need to be every bit as familiar with the Bible, theology and the things of the Spirit as anyone else, and then familiar with how children think and learn as well. Being 'good with children' is nowhere near enough.

So what's the curriculum? Greater power in physical healing, including greater sensitivity about the real nature of the problem (which, as any GP or therapist will tell you, can be very different from that which is presented); an understanding of inner healing and dealing with hurts, sins or traumas from the past that are having a detrimental effect on life in the present; skill in listening to God so that prayer is pin-pointed and focused rather than vague and general; patience and persistence; the ability to deal lovingly and respectfully with those for whom you pray; knowledge of spiritual warfare, and the power of forgiveness and absolution; knowing when to use things like oil or holy water. All these and more will be areas for the leaders to explore and learn about so that they become at least to some degree experts in them.

Then what about children? We've already mentioned that they have fewer theological hang-ups, and that if a Bible story tells them that Jesus healed someone, then he did, and if he did, he still can. So we won't put our fears, hesitations and theological questions onto them, but we'll try to do what Jesus told us and become more like them in their simplicity of faith. We also know that children think much more pictorially than theoretically, so we will explain and teach in more concrete terms, and use images and illustrations that will relate to their world. We will know if we've worked with children for more than five minutes that they have a shorter concentration span than we do, so we won't expect them to feel happy with long periods of silent prayer, and we won't be surprised or offended if they lose interest and wander off after a while. Any children's leader worth their salt will build this understanding into all they try to teach, and the healing ministry needs to be treated in exactly the same way.

The issue of the integration of prayer ministry into the life and worship of your church is a huge one and beyond the scope of this book.[3] But another of Captain Alan's methods of working can provide a helpful way for children to be given space and permission to minister during an all-age service. He calls it '50–50', and he divides the congregation into two halves. One half first of all prays for God to bless the other half, who wait and receive. As they see the Spirit begin to touch people, both adults and children can move over and begin to lay hands on people and bless what God is doing. After a while the half who have received bless the other half in the same way. This may sound outrageous and way beyond what your congregation will handle, but my experience is that generally people find this gentle way of praying acceptable and helpful, particularly if children are involved. Adults have spoken of feeling humbled as the children have prayed for them, and children feel privileged to be allowed to be involved in this way.

That's the nice part, then. But what about when it isn't quite so perfect? We'll move on in the next chapter to look at helping children cope with failure and death.

---

[3] John Leach, *Developing Prayer Ministry* (Grove, 2000) is an attempt to tackle this subject.

8

Failure, Death and Demons

I wouldn't want you to have got the wrong impression from reading the last chapter. In fact you might have got either one of two wrong impressions: that I am tremendously successful at the healing ministry (I'm not), or that since I'm not tremendously successful at it but still want to teach it to children, I'm living in a kind of triumphalistic cloud-cuckoo land (I'm not, but I do believe in Christ's triumph, and I'd rather live with that than the pessimism of some sections of the church). In fact, as I come to address the question of failure, I can say with some honesty that this is a subject I know a lot about, having had quite a lot of experience in it.

This area is a huge issue for adults. Some schools of thought would want to put 'failure' in inverted commas, since nothing is really failure as far as God is concerned. Others (like me) would want to say that if we've asked for someone to get out of their wheelchair and walk and they haven't, it's the closest thing to failure we've ever experienced! If that isn't failure, I'm not quite sure what is! So all sorts of questions spring up to get us, like: 'Whose failure was it?', 'Why do we fail?', 'Does God ever fail?' and, at a deeper level,

'What does it say about people that they find the concept of having failed so distressing that they need to put it in inverted commas to pretend it hasn't happened really?'

Children seem to have no such traumas. Perhaps it is because they fail all the time, and are quite used to it. 'Mummy, can I have some sweets?' comes the question when Mummy pops into the newsagent's for her *Radio Times*. 'No, not today,' comes the reply. This is total and abject failure. The child wants sweets and has failed entirely, 100 per cent, to get any. Not a single sweet. Zilch. Let's face it – that's what most of us would call failure. But children do seem to be very good at being philosophical about it. Rarely do they go into a deep depression and doubt whether, in fact, Mummy really exists at all. Seldom does this kind of event lead them to question the love of their mum, or her power to give them some sweets if it be her will. They seem to be very good at forgetting the whole incident completely in a few minutes (unless of course their parents have trained them into whining and grizzling until they get what they want), and neither does it put them off asking the self-same question next time they're in the newsagent's. Were they able to articulate it, they'd probably tell you that Mummy did love them, but chose not to give them what they wanted there and then for any number of unspecified reasons that they might or might not understand.

Now I'm not wanting to illustrate a God who is whimsical and who sometimes withholds from us things we'd like for reasons we don't understand. It's much more complex than that. I simply want to make the point that not getting what they want is part and parcel of a child's life, and quite honestly it's no big deal. So much of our agonised adult theologising about failure in the healing ministry is irrelevant to them. But there are things we can helpfully say, not in order to explain their mistakes but to encourage persistence.

I try to teach children about the kingdom of God and the battle that is going on as it breaks into our world. We might talk about the Enemy, the prince of this world, who keeps people locked up in a prison, hurts them and frightens them, but we also talk about Jesus, the rightful King, who has come back to fight him, to release those he's locked up, and get them into his army so that they can help release even more people. To avoid dualism I'd make it clear that the castle has been stormed and the Enemy bound up, but that the fighting still goes on until that day when Jesus' victory will be complete. So every time we pray for healing we're fighting a battle, and there's an Enemy who doesn't want Billy's arm to get better because he rather enjoys people hurting and, anyway, he doesn't want Jesus getting any more glory. Then we might talk about why soldiers on earth might lose a battle from time to time: they're too tired or worn out; they don't know how to use their weapons properly; they're too busy fighting among themselves to fight the enemy; they're not listening to their orders well enough, and so on.

When a football team is knocked out of a championship, someone somewhere has to ask why. Perhaps they couldn't get their passing together; they didn't take enough risks; they didn't have the right players in the right place at the right time; perhaps they did all this and the other side were simply stronger on the day. So what might they do? Keep trying and get better at it in time for the next competition. This seems to me a perfectly good and biblical theology of failure, with the added advantage that it is very pictorial and accessible to youngsters. And above all they can be taught that however much they fail, God still loves them, is for them, and wants them to get back into the battle. So when healing does come they can be taught to rejoice and thank God for it, and when it doesn't they can be taught to take it in their stride and keep going. If we feel devastated, we mustn't let it show too much.

Along with failure comes the whole area of death. In a previous parish we struggled in prayer over a little boy of two who had a brain tumour. The battle seemed to ebb and flow for months, with remission and relapse, successful therapy and impossible surgery. Then finally Richard's condition deteriorated and a few days later he died, on our Steve's fourth birthday. He had been a regular member of the children's group, so it was natural that lots of his little friends should be at the funeral, joining in with his favourite songs, like 'God's not dead'.

Another church we know had a similar battle over a boy of 14, also with a brain tumour. For six months the church prayed, and a regular prayer meeting for the children took place (at their request), but finally he too died, on Good Friday at 3 p.m. as it happened, and the shock waves rocked the whole life of the church for some time. So what about children? Is it a danger to their faith to get their expectations up and then find that God doesn't deliver the goods? After all, the one advantage of a liberal interpretation of the Bible with no miracles is that there are no disappointments either. How do we deal in a charismatic way with children and death?

First of all we'd surely want to teach our children that death is real, that it's a fact of life, and that we'll all face it, in others first and then finally for ourselves. Neither would we want to stifle the grieving process, which is every bit as important for children as it is for adults, if somewhat shorter. So death, and especially the death of someone for whom they've prayed, is a real tragedy as far as we are concerned.

But it is my experience that if they are allowed to talk openly about it, children quickly become very philosophical about loss. They can usually talk in quite a matter-of-fact way about their little sister who died – it doesn't seem to be a very big deal. John's experience in schools work is that children are glad to tell the class any stories they have about loss. So our task as children's work leaders is to overcome our natural adult reluctance and encourage the subject to be aired. There will be times when it may be difficult for us personally, but if the children do see us shedding a tear or two it won't harm them; we can tell our story and it'll bring us all closer and teach them some valuable lessons, which may help prevent them clamming up emotionally when they grow up.

Spiritually, we find that most children have a certainty about the fact that their dead friend or relative is now with Jesus, especially in the case of a dead baby or child. It seems almost as if there is an instinctive faith in them, which of course I've argued that there is. Even the children of non-Christian parents have such a certainty. They may have been told so by their parents in order to comfort them, and the parents may or may not actually believe it for themselves, however much they'd like to be able to, but this is one occasion where folk religion is a positive thing, and can reinforce the children's natural faith. If they've prayed and seen death nevertheless, they seem to take that in their stride too. I'd like to be able to tell you exactly how to cope with their devastation and answer all the agonising theological questions, but I'm afraid I can't – I've never had to. It seems to be only adults who get into a mess with things like that. 'God chose not to heal him because he had a better plan,' said one teenager. 'He chose him to go and be with him instead.'

'Disappointment but not devastation' was how the reaction of the children was described by a church leader after their failure to see the 14-year-old healed. 'God knows better than we do, so we don't have to question. He's gone to be with Jesus, so we don't have anything to be sad about any more.' The fact that he had died at exactly the day and time of Jesus' death was of great significance to the children. There was not the slightest trace of them losing faith, being angry with God or asking agonised questions. Instead there was a joy that God's will had been worked out, and paradoxically a new determination to learn to pray better in the future. Only adults, it seems, have big problems with death.

But there is one more area around this subject where adults have a tremendous amount to learn from children. When I originally wrote this part John and I discussed with our boys (then aged nine and eleven) their views on death, and the thing that shone through all their answers was the certainty that life with Jesus is a lot better than life on earth now. While this may reflect their feelings about being a vicarage family, it also suggests that they really do take seriously what the Bible says about heaven, and it really challenges most of the earth-bound Christianity we see lived out in our churches. 'For to me,' said St Paul, 'to live is Christ and to die is gain . . . I desire to depart and be with Christ, which is better by far' (Philippians 1:21, 23). Children really do seem to believe that this is true. As we get older, it appears, we become more and more tangled up in this life, more and more reluctant to leave it, and more and more upset about those who have. Children have so much to teach us about freedom in this area, and they really do believe that their little friends who have died are having a much better time than they are.

One final area concerns the demonic. I believe in the reality of the devil and his minions, because the Bible and my own experience have convinced me of it. Unlike some Christians I'm not that interested in gaining more and more esoteric information about the Enemy, and I certainly don't want to teach children things that go beyond what the Bible teaches, but neither can we ignore this whole subject – the Bible certainly doesn't. So does it impinge on our ministry to children?

And is it something so awful that we need to keep them right away from it?[1]

Some theology and Greek to begin with might be in order. 'Demon possession' is a term that needs to be banned from our vocabulary. It is not a term that has any Greek or Hebrew antecedents, and its common use, even in translations of the Bible that ought to know better, has told us two very big lies about spiritual warfare. The first is that the only thing demons do to people is make them roll around on the floor screaming and foaming at the mouth. The second is that since this kind of behaviour is pretty rare in most churches, so are demons. Neither of these has any basis in fact. So we have a rather different theology, based on the fact that the Greek word *daimonizomai*, used in the New Testament, can best be translated 'demonised' or 'demon-influenced'. How do Satan and demons influence us? In all sorts of ways, very few of which result in teeth-marks on the church pews.

When we're tempted, for example, and give in, we have been influenced by demons. To know this is incredibly liberating, because all at once we realise that everyone is demonised. This isn't some loony lurking in a graveyard; it's me, and I'm still here to tell the tale! Demons can oppress us with doubts and fears, can cause physical illness, can lie to us and make us believe it and, yes, in some extreme cases can cause us to react violently and obscenely against the presence of Jesus. But there's a spectrum. In all the Gospels there is only one occasion when Jesus met what we would think of as

[1] Personally I feel that Nigel Wright, *The Fair Face of Evil* (Marshall Pickering, 1989) is the most healthy book to have been written on spiritual warfare. Those who would hold the opposite view can see it taken to extremes in Frank and Ida Mae Hammond, *Pigs in the Parlour* (New Wine, 1992).

a classically 'demon-possessed' man, with dramatic results (especially for the pig farmer – imagine him filling in his insurance claim!). Only one incident out of three years' ministry. Yet there were many times when he dealt with the demonic in much more down-to-earth ways; in fact, as the writers tell us, 'with a word'.

What this means is that the whole area of deliverance is no big deal. If you were a GP, you'd spend the vast majority of your time on conditions that could be dealt with simply by a few pills, a day or two off work, or a quick jab. Occasionally you'd come across something much more serious, and your job would be to recognise it, but not necessarily to treat it. There are specially trained consultants for that. In the same way most of the demonisation you'll come across will be routine stuff which a quick prayer or command will deal with perfectly well, and there is no reason whatsoever why children can't be involved in this kind of basic ministry as long as they are working alongside a trained adult who not only has some skill and experience in deliverance ministry but can also be sensitive to the children. This kind of apprenticeship training is the way that children learn all sorts of things in life. You'll have to recognise more serious situations, and have some basic knowledge of how to deal with them, but even more important you will have to know when you need to get in an expert. These more serious situations, however, won't crop up that often, or at least if they do you'll begin to ask whether God might be giving you a special ministry!

It is clear from the New Testament that Jesus ministered deliverance to children, and it is likely that children were around while he was doing so. On one occasion (Matthew 15:21–28) he did so from a distance, and on another (Mark 9:14–29) there was direct ministry, again at the request of a parent, and quite a dramatic manifestation of the demonic before the boy was finally set free.

We have occasionally prayed for children directly for deliverance, but most often we've experienced the power of God to set them free without their ever having known anything about the ministry. Praying for them from a distance, and particularly with the agreement of a couple of people in prayer, can be very effective. Some time after our boys were born I found a job in a local school, where I did part-time 'special needs' work. I had previously done a few odd days' supply teaching there, but didn't really know the characters or backgrounds involved. On my first day I was working with a little boy of nine who had reading and behaviour difficulties, when God said to me quite clearly that he had a severe problem with rejection (the boy, not God, although he probably does too if the truth be known). Without James noticing, and without touching him (which of course teachers wouldn't be allowed to do these days), I prayed a silent prayer of deliverance to break the power of rejection over him. From that day on he began to improve. As I found out more about the family background I realised just how right my supernatural information had been, and at his case conference at the end of the year no one could understand why there had been such a dramatic improvement, which went far beyond anything that could have been projected for him.

Another incident involved prayer from a distance with another teacher from the church we were in at the time who was also a member of our healing team. In her class was a girl who showed severe and bizarre temper tantrums. She was always rude and unco-operative, but if told off even mildly she would fly into a rage, and on one occasion she began throwing chairs around the classroom, endangering other children. And even if she was not disciplined, she would have a tantrum every day at 3.20 p.m. just before school ended, when the teacher spent a few moments with the class praying (you can just about get away with that in a church school). The behaviour would get worse whenever they prayed, or in RE lessons, or on the occasional trips to the church. Her teacher felt torn: she didn't want to let her rule and get away without discipline, but at the same time another child might be injured if she provoked a violent episode. The rules about physical contact with children hampered her severely too. Finally, knowing my involvement in this area, she sought my advice. Could there be something demonic in Jennifer's background which made her act in such antisocial ways? The two of us decided to pray together about it.

We handled the session exactly as we would have done had we been faced with a person asking for deliverance, but without Jennifer actually being present. We invited the Spirit to come on her, wherever she was, and asked God for words of knowledge about what was going on. He spoke clearly to us, particularly about her birth and her father, now long gone. We prayed over these issues, just as we would have done had she been there with us, asking Jesus to go back in time and minister to the hurts and pains, and bring forgiveness for the sins involved, and then we broke any demonic power attached to her birth or her family lines. When we felt a sense of peace, we stopped.

There was an immediate difference, and the 3.20 tantrums stopped almost straight away. The other violent behaviour patterns gradually subsided over the next few months, and Jennifer became not perfect but reasonably normal. She would still throw a wobbly now and then, but not that much more than any of the other children in the class, and she could be disciplined for doing so. Further exploration of the family background revealed all sorts of evil influences, and sadly there is not yet complete freedom, and neither will there be until there is repentance or until Jennifer leaves the family environment, but at least the manifestations are being kept under control and other children are safer.

Quite apart from what it did for Jennifer, the incident helped the teacher. Perhaps without being fully aware of it she had been in a battle for some time, and she realised that she had been, in *Ghostbusters* terminology, well and truly 'slimed'. She had been suffering from frequent headaches, and often felt a real sense of heavy oppression over her. She came to realise that her presence with Jennifer, and in particular her attempts to bring Jesus into the classroom with her, had caused her to be the subject of attack herself. Other members of the healing team were able to set her free from this, and her physical symptoms stopped immediately.

Deliverance ministry isn't something for the complete novice, but with a bit of training and experience you can easily begin to pray for children whom you suspect may be troubled in this way. Of course you need some indication that the demonic is involved before you begin praying, but if you suspect anything, it may be that dramatic results will follow your ministry. And as far as I know, no one has yet phoned Childline to complain that they're being prayed for, especially if you follow the good example of praying over them from a distance or while they're asleep.

There isn't space here to go into the ways of recognising and discerning the presence of the demonic, and the books mentioned previously will give enough details to those who are unfamiliar with this ministry. Children, if present for the ministry, need be treated no differently from adults in principle, but involving the parents wherever possible (as Jesus did in our two examples) is helpful, as is a full explanation of what is going on. Fear is learned, and if children see you go into a panic when one of their number reacts dramatically to the presence of the Spirit during a worship time, they will get the message that this is terrifying. But if they see you react calmly and confidently, if you invite them to minister along with you, and if you explain clearly to them what is going on, and above all if you keep smiling all the time and don't get too heavy about it all, they'll soon learn that this is all a part of following Jesus and take it in their stride. Children have a tremendous capacity for coping, and it is tragic that so often we infect them with our fear, insecurity and doubt. The whole area of healing and deliverance provides adults with a fresh challenge to obey Jesus' words and become like little children. Let's make sure it doesn't go the other way and we make them become like us.

9
Children and the Bible

I've tried to emphasise all along that I regard the Bible as the supreme authority in the church. The gifts of the Spirit are not to be seen in any way as in competition with Scripture, but rather the two complement each other as the Spirit illuminates the word and the word provides parameters for the Spirit. How can we teach our children to value both word and Spirit, and live fully in the light of what God has said and what he says now?

Let's begin by looking at some of the symptoms of neglect of one side or the other of this equation. Everyone is familiar with the manifestations of unbridled charismania; you have only to read the Corinthian correspondence to see it in action. The addiction to experience; the lack of spiritual discipline; the selfishness that masquerades as spirituality; the playing down of the importance of a holy lifestyle; empire-building through a divine hotline; lack of submission to leaders; triumphalism that marginalises those experiencing suffering and pain: all these are as common in the church today as they were in Corinth. Indeed there is special danger in a culture as concerned as ours is with the pursuit of pleasure and experience for those who major on the supernatural gifts of the Spirit. It is very easy to make charismatic Christianity look like yet another New Age trip.

But the other side of the equation, which is less well known but just as nasty, is worth looking at. David Watson described what he called 'textualism', quoting Tozer, who defined it as 'orthodoxy without the Holy Ghost'. He continues to quote:

> Everywhere among conservatives we find persons who are Bible-taught but not Spirit-taught . . . Truth that is not experienced is no better than error, and may be fully as dangerous. The scribes who sat in Moses' seat were not the victims of error; they were the victims of their failure to experience the truth they taught.

Watson goes on: 'Until the Holy Spirit illuminates our dull minds and warms our cold hearts, we do not receive God's revealed truth, no matter how accurately we know the right words and teach them to others.'[1]

Richard Wurmbrand once pointed out that in communist prisons he found Christians who knew Bible verses such as 'My grace is sufficient for you', but they found little comfort in these verses alone. It is God's grace that is sufficient for us, not verses about it.

If charismania was the presenting problem in one book of the Bible, textualism runs throughout many. 'These people come near to me with their mouth and honour me with their lips,' said Isaiah (29:13), 'but their hearts are far from me.' In Psalm 50:16 we read, 'But to the wicked, God says: "What right have you to recite my laws or take my covenant on your lips? You hate my instruction and cast my words behind

---

[1] D. Watson, *Discipleship* (Hodder & Stoughton, 1981), p. 145.

you."' Jesus picked up verses like these and used them against the scribes and Pharisees, who epitomised those who love the words of the Law but miss their spirit entirely. Matthew 23 contains devastating criticism of those who were so zealous for the letter of the Law that they missed out on the very things the Law taught about the inner life and the fruit of the Spirit. We can see in other passages too Jesus' attack on the self-same shibboleths that the evangelical world is still arguing about today: the use of Sunday (Matthew 12:1–14), whether or not 'signs and wonders' can be authenticated empirically (12:38–39 and 16:1–4), what you eat (and perhaps drink or smoke?) (15:1–20), divorce (19:1–12), and so much more. It's not that these things don't matter – on the contrary, Jesus' followers must be every bit as holy as the Pharisees, and a lot more besides (Matthew 5:20), and they must be as committed to Scripture as those who are renowned for teaching it (5:17–19) – it's just that there are weightier matters to consider too. For all their theology and commitment to the word, the scribes simply didn't recognise the work of God when they saw it. 'You diligently study the Scriptures because you think that by them you possess eternal life,' said Jesus to the Jewish leaders. 'These are the Scriptures that testify about me, yet you refuse to come to me to have life' (John 5:39–40). It requires a particular degree of spiritual deadness to see the power of Jesus and call it the devil at work, but even this was done in the Bible (Matthew 12:22–32), and tragically has been done in today's church too. It is interesting to observe the reaction of some of those from certain sections of the church if they are asked to consider whether some of these criticisms might validly be applied to them. There is often a bristling self-righteousness that looks pretty similar to the self-righteousness Jesus was greeted with.

The point is, you see, that the sharp cutting edge of the

word needs to be sheathed sometimes in the bejewelled scabbard of the Spirit. There are times to go on the offensive, and to wield the sword for truth and righteousness, but there are also times to put it away and use love and beauty instead. It seems to be an observable fact in the church that those who are most zealous for the Scriptures can be those who have a hard, cold edge to them which is as profoundly unattractive today as it was in Jesus' time. It was the lawyers and Pharisees who dragged a woman from her lover's bed to Jesus for condemnation, and legally they had every right to do so, but Jesus chose the way of grace instead, no doubt much to their annoyance (John 8:1–11). I'm not arguing for spiritual laxity, any more than Jesus was spiritually lax on that occasion, but rather for the meeting of law and grace, of righteousness and love. 'Love and faithfulness meet together,' declared the psalmist. 'Righteousness and peace kiss each other' (Psalm 85:10). It is this meeting of faithfulness to Scripture and love given by the Spirit which the church, and in particular its children, desperately needs.

So what does this mean for children's ministry? It means that we must teach not just word and Spirit, but also an understanding of the relationship between them. To clamp down on and denigrate the very spiritual gifts the New Testament urges us earnestly to desire is an incredible example of doublethink. When the author of the letter to the Ephesians enjoins his readers to be filled with the Spirit so that they overflow in worship and praise, he's not talking to a group of weirdos on the fringe of the church somewhere: this is mainstream biblical Christianity. How can we disobey, teach others to disobey and then claim to be biblical? It's a nonsense, and our children will see right through it, even if we can't. An adage from the early days of renewal is still appropriate: 'Word only – you dry up; Spirit only – you blow up; word and Spirit – you grow up'. This balance is essential if children are to grow up avoiding the extremes of pharisaical evangelicalism or loony charismania.

The same is true for those from another branch of the church who would want to edit out of the Bible everything they, with their Enlightenment mindset, consider to be unacceptable, like miracles, healings, resurrection and so on. Children haven't yet become sophisticated enough to play clever adult mind games. If they read something they treat it either as a fairy story or as truth. If it's truth, they'll begin to ask sooner or later where it is in their own experience and the experience of the church. If they can see it, all well and good, but if not, the credibility of the whole Bible will go out of the window. If on the other hand they're taught that it's a fairy story, they will probably grow out of it and abandon their faith as a passing phase. As we've already seen, hundreds of youngsters continue weekly to go down this path.

Now you may be thinking that this is a recipe for fundamentalism, and you may quite simply be intellectually unable to accept such a position. Good – so am I. But it's all a question of what you're fundamentalist about, and this leads us onto another subject: children and hermeneutics. Hermeneutics is the branch of theology that deals with the ways in which we interpret the Bible for today, and it is arguably the most important branch of theology there is. Children, I believe, need to be taught not just that the Bible is there, important and real; they need also to be given some clue as to how to understand it, and how it can appropriately be applied to life a few thousand years on from when it was written. This is obviously a massive subject, and even I can't claim to have a major grasp of it myself, but I do try to tell children in my care that the subject exists, and I attempt to help them begin to understand the questions, even if not all the answers.

Many children who are exposed to the Bible imbibe the view (often by default in the absence of anything else to go on) that it dropped out of heaven one day in its finished form. One popular worship song even describes the Bible as 'the book which came from heaven', a phrase which can't help but reinforce that view! Nowadays, however, most Christians would have an understanding that there is a bit more to it than that, and they would be aware of some of the things the theologians spend their time doing with ancient manuscripts and versions. They would also know that there were at least questions about the authorship and dating of some of the books, even if they couldn't find their way through the technical arguments involved. But how often do we bring our children in on this kind of discussion? There seems to be an unarticulated fear lurking around the minds of leaders that biblical theology, criticism and interpretation is X-rated stuff for adults only. Why this fear? Because many Christians were brought up, either as children or as new adult Christians, with the same naïve oblivion to the questions I've already mentioned. When they first encountered them the shock was great, and they've responded often by putting all such things on one side as too intellectually difficult and too threatening to the belief that 'this is the word of the Lord'. So they feel that to expose mere children to such unsettling questions would do them irreparable harm.

Is it possible to do degree-level theology with five-year-olds? In a way it is. We need to be honest in what we teach, and admit when we don't know something. To make children aware that there are questions and uncertainties, but that they're not that crucial, is a vital work. It isn't an undermining of the supreme authority of the Bible; it's just honesty. For children the Bible will be authoritative when they see their parents and leaders loving it, valuing it, using it and obeying it. Questions about who actually wrote it are secondary. We may be unclear or agnostic about the authorship of certain books, and we may explain that fact to our children, but the real issue is whether or not we live out its teaching.

Now of course this approach may sound dangerously liberal to some, or suspiciously like wanting to have our cake and eat it to others. How can we possibly be so certain about the reality of the supernatural on the one hand and yet be so agnostic about the text on the other? Aren't we trying to be liberal and fundamentalist at the same time, and won't that confuse our children beyond their ability to cope? No, and the reason is this: some things we can't know, so we don't worry too much about them, but some things we can, so we'll concentrate on them. Who wrote the various parts of the Old Testament? We admit we don't always know. We're looking forward to that day when we find out, but for now we're quite honestly not that bothered. But speaking in tongues? Yes, it's real, here and now; Paul would love us all to do it, so here we go. See the difference? It's about sorting out the intellectual questions from the practical ones; it's about obedience. And with children it's about not letting them get the impression things are sewn up when we really can't be that sure, but neither must we allow them to miss out on what God the Holy Spirit has for them.

So how might this work out in practice? I'll end this chapter with four brief headings, under each of which will be an actual case study of something we've done to work out these principles.

Socialising

This is a term that refers to the fact that we learn as much by being with the right people as we do from studying the right material. Medical students, for example, tend to behave in certain ways because they've learned to do so by being with other medical students. This is a recognised sociological phenomenon, and it applies all over the place, from senior common rooms to antenatal clinics. So we can use it to our (and the children's) advantage by seeking deliberately to create a climate where the Bible is valued and used. It was my policy when I worked in our parish church to present to the children, as soon as they entered our 6–11s group, a Good News Bible and a set of Bible reading notes appropriate to their age. There was from time to time teaching about regular Bible reading, but far more often there was just the tacit assumption that as Christians we will read the Bible. So we talked about what people had been reading over the past week, how God had spoken to them and so on. And we expected the children to turn up on Sundays with their Bibles, for those times when we would look at a passage together. The socialisation seemed to do as much good as the more direct teaching.

Memorising

I believe it is important to learn Bible verses off by heart, but I've found that this can be transformed from a dull exercise into a living encounter with God by personalising what the children remember. I mentioned earlier Steve's photo held securely in the hands of God. Another example of this same thing in action was a picture of a soldier in armour, again drawn by a talented artist, with the words 'Steve – put on all the armour that God gives you' written colourfully across it. This too became a treasured bedroom ornament which provided a reminder each day.

This same approach can be used to make the words of the Bible more accessible to youngsters. 'Go throughout the whole world and preach the gospel to all mankind' is a big challenge by anyone's standards, but if it can be altered slightly to read 'Go throughout Grange Farm School and preach the gospel' it immediately becomes something much more within reach. After all, it's good to begin small. They can move on to the rest of the world once they've learned to cross the road.

Another tremendously powerful aid to memorising is the use of Scripture songs. There is a vast quantity of material by Ishmael and others which the children love to sing. The songs are simple enough to be picked up and learned quickly, and they stay in the children's heads throughout the week, thus constantly feeding them with God's word. Not only this; there are even songs like 'Have you got an appetite?' which, rather than just being a setting of a verse from the Bible, is about the value of feeding on the Bible. Children love these songs, and they really do help Scripture to get in and stay in. And if there isn't a song for the particular verse you're wanting to use, why not write your own? You'd be amazed at how easy it can be. Many parents have done this instinctively with young children.

Studying

An interesting series we taught in our children's groups was designed to introduce children to some of the ideas behind hermeneutical issues. It began by the leaders finding examples of different types of literature from everyday life. One brought a thank-you letter to Auntie Mabel for the lovely scarf, and another read a nursery rhyme. There was also a section from a history book, and a bit of the *Highway Code*, and so on. As each was read out, the children had to identify what type of writing it was.

Then followed some teaching about the inappropriateness of confusing different types and using them for the wrong purpose; for example thanking Auntie Mabel by telling her not to overtake near a humpback bridge, or asking the exact date and time of the cow's jump over the moon, and how it had managed such an incredible feat of aerodynamics. As you can imagine this was great fun. But it led on to a serious discussion, illustrated from different parts of the Bible, about the need to be every bit as discerning about what we do with what we read. We can get into just as much of a mess if we misunderstand how the different genres in the Bible work, and what exactly they're meant to tell us. This was then applied practically with some work on how we might respond to different styles: we'd obey commands, worship through poetic passages, and so on. Thus the children were introduced, in a fun and accessible way, to some teaching that many fundamentalist adults have never mastered!

Applying

While I certainly intend everything I do with the Bible to be applicable to real life, it is still possible to have sessions where we particularly work on this. I have found it a good principle to make sure that the children's themes each week tie in with those of the adult teaching series, although the level of application will obviously be different. We went through a period where John felt that God had told him to preach through the book of Haggai. The church was at a stage where it needed consciously to switch from tinkering with its own internal structures to turning inside out to make outreach the priority; to stop making home improvements in its panelled houses and start building the temple of the Lord. So the children too studied Haggai during this period, at their own level.

First of all there was some background teaching which told

the children that this wasn't just a story, it was about a real person who lived at a real time in a real place. What would it have been like to have lived then? All sorts of background information was taught in a way that helped the children to step in their imagination into the prophet's world. The next session simply made the point that in a time when everyone was very busy with their own interests, Haggai heard God. This allowed a recap on how we hear God ('You see it, you hear it, you feel it, you know it, you say it'), plus some teaching on the fact that if we are going to hear God speaking to us we need to slow down and give him space and time. Quite naturally a practical session followed, where the Spirit came and the children listened and shared prophetic words and pictures.

The next week we talked about obedience: Haggai's to God, and the people's to Haggai. And so it went on. Hermeneutical questions were not ignored, the work of the Spirit was built in, and the teaching was applied to the children's own personal lives. This kind of approach, which takes seriously intellect and experience, is not impossible with young children. It just means that the leaders have to be a bit more theologically clued up and imaginative. But then children's work is never the easy option!

10

Children in the Church

So far I have only alluded to the role of the whole church in
children's ministry. Now we must look at this subject in more
detail, because although the children's ministry can have an
important effect in leading youngsters into the things of the
Spirit, it doesn't happen in isolation. I can remember our boys
learning in their science lessons about the 'fire triangle'.
Burning can only take place where there are three ingredients
present: fuel, oxygen and heat. Take any one of them away
and the fire can't keep going. This can provide a useful picture of the fire of God's Spirit at work in the lives of children:
there is in fact a three-way partnership, between the children's
work, the church as a whole and the human family. If one of
these is ignorant of or closed to the work of the Spirit, the
children's experience will die down and merely smoulder,
when what we really want is for them to be well and truly on
fire for the Lord.

This chapter is about the church side of this triangle. I have
known churches where the children's work was going great
guns, but the church itself had a positively mediaeval attitude
towards it. However good the time is children spend in their

139

own groups, they will pick up clear messages from the time they spend with the whole church, and if the messages contradict each other, a tension will be set up within the children. How can we make these 'church' messages positive rather than negative? The answer has to do with rights and responsibilities.

In 1989 the Children Act became law in Britain. Into a climate of growing awareness (if not necessarily growing incidence) of all kinds of child abuse, this new legislation sought to recognise that children are people too, and they have just as many rights as adults. This seemed at the time a very positive step, but now increasingly we are seeing what one journalist calls 'the curious philosophy behind it, which is now suddenly coming home to roost'. Commenting on the sharp rise in false accusations aimed by children at their teachers, she asks, 'What on earth did we mean when we decided children should in effect be treated as if they were adults, with full rights? . . . what do we mean by rights for those too young to take adult responsibility?'[1] Many have likened oppressed and abused children to other oppressed minority groups in society, but there is one major difference. If someone is a woman, or black, they are fairly likely to remain so for the rest of their life. Their oppressors are presumably not women or black, and therefore have no idea how it feels, hence the oppression. But children are different. Being a child is a temporary phase, a phase through which all of us adults have passed. Any attempt to deal with children's rights must take this significant difference into account.

I mention this because there is currently much discussion about the 'rights' of children as members of churches. In the past children certainly were treated in some pretty unhelpful

---

[1] Polly Toynbee, *Radio Times*, 12–18 March 1994.

ways: babies who so much as burped during the service were glared at, there were stewards or churchwardens ready to ask parents to control their noisy offspring, or even to remove them. Children who did stay were ignored, or patronised with a two-minute 'children's address'. They were given no books from which to follow the service, and were seldom greeted at the door by those on duty. Many young families, seeing this passive or even active hostility, were frightened away from church altogether, as the number of congregations nowadays with no one aged under 60 shows.

But now it's all different. Children are, as I've said, the church of today, and they have rights, just as any member does. They have the right to have their say in a service, even if it is at a quiet moment and even if it does disrupt the worship of a couple of hundred other people. They have the right to wander about without restraint, to wrap themselves round the minister's leg while he or she is preaching, to travel three-toed-sloth-style along the altar rail singing school assembly folk songs while others are trying to receive communion, and swing from the altar cloth, bringing communion vessels down on their heads, while their parents smile benignly from their seats, celebrating their children's freedom and the wonderful church's relaxed attitude towards them. Meanwhile, many older people, who no longer feel the church is giving them their rights to a reverent and well-managed service, exercise their right to stay away instead.

Something has gone wrong, as any teacher will tell you. The pendulum has swung too far, and the church, as well as the state, is confused over how to behave. Just what are children's rights, and how do they work within the church family? And how can the correct handling of this area facilitate the work of the Spirit in their young lives?

The simple answer, surely, is that they have the right to a

church that treats them as God would treat them, and just as their human parents should treat them. I'll suggest six ways in which this right must be worked out, and then move on to the other side of the coin: their responsibilities.

1. The right to be understood

I've argued already that the children in our care are to be helped to grow in the fruit and gifts of the Spirit, to become more and more aware of their inheritance as children of God, and to be protected against the forces that would teach them to devalue that inheritance and drag them away from it. But how do children grow? I've said that we should be providing for them both intellectual information about God and practical experience of him, but in order to avoid treating them inappropriately we need to have some understanding of their psychology and spirituality. By learning about their needs, we may be in a better position to lead them on.

Two important studies of this subject have been done by John Westerhoff[2] and James Fowler.[3] As you might expect with scholarly studies they reach different conclusions, but they agree in saying that children develop their faith through different stages. A useful summary of their work can be found in an Anglican General Synod report entitled *Children in the Way*,[4] but it is worth outlining it even more briefly here, in order to see how it fits with our philosophy of discipling children.

---

[2] J. H. Westerhoff III, *Will Our Children Have Faith?* (Seabury, 1980) and *Bringing Up Children in the Christian Faith* (Harper and Row, 1980).

[3] J. Fowler, *Stages of Faith* (Harper and Row, 1989), and *Becoming Adult, Becoming Christian* (Harper and Row, 1984).

[4] *Children in the Way* (The National Society/Church House Publishing, 1988), pp. 38ff.

Westerhoff's model is the simpler, with four stages. Children begin, he claims, with an 'experienced faith', based not on what we tell them about Christianity but on how adults are as Christians with their children. They sense, explore, observe and copy the stimuli around them, and experience through interaction. Next comes the stage of 'affiliative faith'. Here, belonging is important, and membership of a community of faith that consciously identifies itself as such is vital. The child joins in the activities of the community, listens to its stories and shares something of the awe and mystery holding the community together. The child needs to be accepted and to feel a sense of togetherness, and will take on board much that a significant and trusted leader gives to them, often in the context of a peer group, which is also trusted.

The child then enters a 'searching faith' phase, where he or she will question, experiment, look at other points of view, and finally arrive at a faith that works because it makes sense to them, rather than because someone else has taught them to believe it. This in turn leads to an 'owned faith', which is a mature holding together of different approaches (while maintaining a commitment to one) along with a new appreciation of the myth, symbolism and ritual of the church. Arriving here (and this arrival is what Westerhoff calls 'conversion') enables the Christian to make a stand for their faith, even when doing so alienates them to some degree from the community in which they have grown up.

Fowler's analysis of the same journey is more complex (and uses even longer words), but the main ideas are not incompatible with Westerhoff's. His first stage, the 'Primal' phase, is one in which the child sees his or her parents as 'super-ordinate power and wisdom' (that means they're like God). This soon gives way to the 'Intuitive–Projective' phase, where the child moves to a joining in with the stories, sym-

bols and rituals of the faith. Then he moves on to the third
stage of 'Mythic–Literal' faith, where the stories and rules of
the family are valued, even though they don't provide a particularly coherent meaning for life. Next comes the
'Synthetic–Conventional' phase, where some of these elements are put together with the child's own life experience in
the search for an overall meaning. The fifth stage is that of
'Individuative–Reflective' faith, where a conscious awareness
of having a belief system different from that of others is
developed – an awareness that is capable of articulation in
abstract terms. This stage gives way eventually to the next,
that of 'Paradoxical–Consolidative' faith. What happens here
is that many opposing viewpoints are examined fully for the
first time and held in tension with others, until finally the pil-
grim arrives at the climactic seventh 'Universalising' stage,
where (and here only a direct quotation will do) 'coherence
gives a new simplicity centred on "a oneness beyond but
inclusive of the manyness of Being"'![5] (One wonders whether
there is then a graduation to a whole new level, where begins
the eternal and unending quest for the word 'manyness' in a
self-respecting English dictionary.)

One point needs to be made to do justice to both Westerhoff
and Fowler: although I have used the term 'child' to describe
the plucky traveller through these sinister-sounding regions,
the fact is that age doesn't really come into it all that much.
Many adults have never progressed in their faith past the first
couple of stages, while some children race through as far as
their intellectual capacities will carry them. So it is difficult to
say that a child ought to have got somewhere by a particular
age. It just depends.

Clearly this research is very clever, but the chances are that

[5] *Ibid.*, p. 53.

most of the leaders in your children's ministry will not find it life-changing to any high degree. Is it possible to distil from this some helpful and jargon-free principles that can make our discipling of children more effective?

First of all, both writers agree that faith is a growing, dynamic thing rather than something you haven't got one minute but acquire the next. And while intellectual growth doesn't guarantee spiritual maturity, the lack of it certainly can limit it. A young child simply hasn't got the mental equipment to weigh up opposing views on the authorship and date of the book of Daniel, but he'll love the bit about the lions, because he saw one once in the zoo. This speaks to the anxiety I have mentioned over indoctrination: young children do just need to be told things in order to grasp them.

Second, there is agreement over the need for youngsters to make the faith and belief their own. A period of questioning and indeed of letting go of some things is an important part of the acquisition of mature faith. How much more helpful it is, then, for the child to have experiences of God as well as information about him to weigh up during this questioning phase. It is probably at this stage that most youngsters give up on the church, as they examine and test what they've been told, only to find that there is no empirical evidence for any of it, in their own lives or in the life of their church. Knowing that Jesus was supposed to have healed sick people must inevitably raise sooner or later questions about whether he still does. That question is, as we've said, easier to answer positively if you've seen him do it, or felt him do it to you!

Third, the need throughout the process for an accepting and nurturing community is paramount, and this we will examine more closely in due course, as we try to discover what kind of church community children have 'the right' to. But before we leave them, I have one final reflection on

Westerhoff and Fowler. They clearly do have things of value to teach us, even if we can't always pronounce them! I'm not so sure, however, about the so-called arrivals at the final stage that each describes. Personally I prefer to think of a mature Christian as one who will make a stand for the truth of the faith, rather than as one who has discovered their place in the 'manyness of Being', but then I'm just old-fashioned. But if maturity is, as seems to be implied, a loss of the childlike innocence that just takes God at his word and obeys him, then surely we've got it rather on its head. Jesus told his disciples that they needed to go back a few stages when they thought they'd arrived. Of course a child's faith needs to grow to a level of sophistication beyond that which they could manage when they first joined the crèche, but I'd want to resist any suggestion that maturity is about becoming cleverer than God, and learning to sit in judgement over his word. The gospel way is that while the adults have much to teach children, they have even more to learn from them.

2. The right to be accepted

There is no doubt that children need an accepting community. The earliest stages of growth are not about what children know, but what they feel, and how adults feel about them. So it is the task of every church member to show affection, kindness, welcome and warmth to children. They should be welcomed as they arrive, for example, not just ignored while their parents get a handshake and several books. They shouldn't be glared at or asked to leave if they make the inevitable kinds of noises (or smells) that very young children do make from time to time. They should be given times in the service when they can contribute in their own inimitable way, and even times when the whole thing is geared directly to them, even if it is in the crèche rather than the church. This welcoming attitude is one that children will pick up, but parents will do so even more, and a church that knows how to make children of all ages feel valued is onto a winning formula for growth.

As toddlers grow into children and then into teenagers, the acceptance of the church community becomes progressively more important. Part of growing up is the need to kick against all the rules that have proscribed life until now, to see which ones shift. It is not only parents, but churches as well, that have to develop the unyielding attitude to the truth which can absorb anger and hatred and respond with firmness and love. This can continue long past adolescence, and many a church council will have an 'angry young man' or woman among its number. This can be very healthy for the church if it means that some of its sacred cows are threatened with slaughter, but there will be many cases where youth will have to bow to experience, and youngsters have a right to learn this lesson, which will serve them well in later life. A church community that can deal with the questioning and even hostility of its younger members and respond with the same accepting love it is showing to its babies is a healthy organisation indeed.

Another problem can be the fact that youngsters will realise sooner or later that your church does not have a monopoly on truth, nor is it the only viable option for them, and they may begin to experiment with visits elsewhere. A church must accept this without taking it personally, but at the same time it must work to protect them from wandering outside the parameters of orthodox faith. This is a delicate matter, and a wise church leadership will both appreciate its own limitations and also know where the outside boundaries are. There is a lot of evidence to suggest that most children of Christian parents will grow up to mature membership of a church significantly different from the one in which their parents brought them up, and wise leaders and parents will recognise this phenomenon when they see it and not stand in its way. But at the same time they will try to suggest to their adolescents that the Buddhist temple down the road might not be the best place to continue their Christian discipleship.

3. The right to be valued

I've mentioned in my vision statement the kind of quality we believe the children in our care deserve. The toys they play with; the materials they use; the music they listen to; the adults who look after them and the environment in which they meet: all these can be good or bad, and children are worthy of the best, because the best is what their heavenly Father would want them to have. We don't of course want to fall into the materialistic trap of equating the best with the most expensive, but we do want to avoid any sense of palming the youngsters off with the leftovers no one else wants.

But there is more to this than just material things, important though they are for showing value. As children grow older and become more established in the use of spiritual gifts, they will need to be shown that the church values the contributions they can make. Depending on your style of worship, this may be more or less difficult to manage. If you regularly have people sharing 'from the floor' what they think God is saying, it may be relatively easy for children to gain a hearing. If on the other hand your worship is more heavily controlled from the front, or if your church is simply a large one, it will be far more daunting for anyone, never mind children, to speak up.

When we were in Coventry we had a large morning service, for part of which the children were present, but it was rare that words or pictures were shared, and if they were it was most often done by jotting details down and handing them to the service leader, who would then share what he or she felt appropriate. Children could be included in this if their parents or leaders helped them with the writing, but public speaking in such a daunting context was rarely heard. But we also had another service, later in the day, where specific time was given to waiting to hear God speak. We often built in workshop-type sessions, where people experimented in small groups (rather along the lines of the procedure described in Chapter 5). There were fewer youngsters at this service, but the contributions of those who did come were heard and valued, and children often joined in personal ministry to those who had been touched by the Spirit. So it may not be important for the children to be able to contribute spiritual gifts at every service, as long as there is one somewhere at which they can. The larger the church the harder it is to open things up to the congregation, so look for the smaller contexts and actively encourage children there.

4. The right to be spiritual

As children are set free to contribute in worship, it may dawn on adults that they are indeed spiritual beings, with a spirituality of their own. This should lead to new attitudes towards them. If they're in the crèche or children's group, they're not there just to be taken out of the way while the adults get on with the real serious business. They're there to meet God in a way that is appropriate for them. So we didn't give them *Goldilocks* or *Snow White* to read, since they could get that any time. We gave them little books of Bible stories. We didn't show them *Fireman Sam* videos for the same reason, but we did use material that had spiritual content instead. And we had leaders who saw the job not just as child-minding, but as praying for and talking to the children in a way that communicated the love of God to them.

As they grow, children's spirituality needs to be taken seriously in other ways: the worship will include them and be relevant and appropriate to them, and adults will be happy to make minor sacrifices of style and content for the sake of allowing their spirituality to be expressed. Those who lead the worship will acknowledge the presence of children, steering a course between the twin perils of ignoring them or patronising them. So, for example, they will allow more 'rustling' time when they've announced a Bible reading or piece of liturgy, they'll speak more slowly and clearly when they expect children to join in, and they'll gladly do all the thousand and one other things that a little imagination and the ability to put themselves in smaller-sized shoes will tell them.[6]

5. The right to be disciplined

Church is not just a free-for-all, though. Children have a right to a church that disciplines them. They really do need to know that obedience is expected and enforced within the church family. They need to learn that unbridled self-expression is not their divine right, especially if it interferes with the conflicting rights of others. For their own good they have to learn that it is appropriate sometimes to be quiet and sometimes to be noisy, sometimes to bounce around and sometimes to sit still. On several occasions we have invited them to shout in worship – after all, some of the liturgy demands to be shouted. Grown-ups probably won't do this naturally, but children love it, so we include it. They can also dance more

---

[6] John has written a useful training course for leaders of worship (especially worship at which children are present) called *Leading Worship that Connects* (Lynx, 1999).

easily than most adults, so we let them, without forcing anyone else to join in. But at other times they will need to learn to behave in very different ways. As long as the church provides both sorts of times, it has the right to expect appropriate behaviour at each, and it has the right to expect that parents with young children will gladly co-operate in enforcing this behaviour.

We don't think churchwardens should have to remove noisy children from services, because their parents should know what is acceptable and what isn't and should do the removing themselves. The wardens can then direct them to a quiet spot where the problem can be resolved before rejoining the service. If there is an ongoing problem, the parents may need a quiet talk from someone in the church leadership. On more than one occasion in the past things have become so bad that John as the vicar had to visit families and tell them that they were no longer welcome at services because their children were constantly being so disruptive to the worship of the other couple of hundred people. This is, however, a very last resort, and most parents will gladly help their children to behave if they know what standards are expected and have some help in knowing how to enforce them.

6. The right to be employed

As children grow older, they have the right to expect that they will be accepted by the church family in a way that allows them to contribute something to its life. This may involve being on a 'junior stewards' rota, and helping with the practical tasks of service management; it may, as ability increases, involve taking part in a service as adults do through leading prayers or reading from the Bible. They can be invited to help with all-age talks in one way or another, or to play or sing with a choir or music group. One of the most efficient teams in our church was the overhead projector team, which was run and staffed almost entirely by the youth group. There was always someone there to operate the OHP, they were there in good time, and they did a good job. We simply never had to worry, because it always got done. Sadly the same couldn't be said of other teams, which were run by adults. That wasn't all the youth group did, but they did feel that it was an area where they could hold a sense of ownership, and could make a significant contribution, which they did willingly and well.

The responsibilities

These then are some of the rights God has given to youngsters and which the church must provide for them. But to pretend, as the Children Act seems to, that they are equal to adults in every way is clearly nonsense. It is also wrong, of course, to say that their value to God is any less than that of adults. The bottom line is that they have a right to be treated like children; in other words they should be trained up and nurtured so that when they become adults physically and emotionally they can do so spiritually too. So along with their rights we must also consider their responsibilities.

Your church will no doubt have agreed standards of expectation on its members. In the Free churches these may be high, and they will be less so in an Anglican setting which traditionally welcomes all-comers without much being asked of them. By seeking to discern which standards will be appropriate for children, and working to enforce them, we will be building good foundations for the future.

One example of this has already been mentioned: the responsibility to act in an appropriately reverent manner. This may not mean, as many adults would want to interpret it, *quiet* behaviour, but it will mean a sense of what is appropriate at different times in the service. If children are allowed to shout and dance at one point, they should also be able to be quiet and still at another. In our church the children rejoined the adults during the administration of communion, and they used at first to come whooping and racing into the church at one of the most peaceful and reverent points in the liturgy. Quite naturally some adults found this disruptive, so the leaders talked to the children about it and they soon learned to make their entrance a bit less dramatic, much to everyone's relief.

Another responsibility I have always taught children concerns financial giving. At times when the grown-ups were being taught about this it featured also on the curriculum of all the children's and youth groups. They were taught about tithing, and most of them joined the envelope scheme and gave regularly a tenth of their pocket money, paper-round wages or whatever. In fact they were soon streets ahead of the adults, and about 3 per cent of our church's annual income came from children and youth (I'd be very surprised if they received between them 3 per cent of the total earnings!). To be honest the financial contribution children can make will never actually be that significant as a proportion of a church's total annual turnover, and initially we faced annoyed comments from the envelope counters who had to open and record loads of envelopes with a few pence in each week. One person even worked out the cost of buying offering envelopes and decided that it wasn't worth giving them to children for what they brought back! But it was highly significant spiritually, because when we train children to give we are building for the future and establishing good habits at the very time when they are the most easy to establish. If our adult members had been trained early into tithing we'd have no financial worries at all in the church now!

So responsibility goes hand in hand with rights, and a church that is co-operating with the children's ministry in giving rights and demanding responsibilities will help to keep the fires of the Spirit burning brightly in the young lives of our children. But I must end this chapter with a cautionary note to those working with children who find the church's leadership totally unsympathetic to their direction.

In our particular partnership the children's work leader happened to be married to the vicar, so there was no conflict of vision or direction between the two, even without my resorting to the rolling pin! But sadly that is not always the case. It is not the place of this book to say that a church must have a particular ethos, direction or theology of children. I've simply recommended ours, but yours is a matter between the leadership and God.

But I would want to say this: don't lead children's work in defiance of the leadership in a direction they do not approve of. However good it may seem, you will be doing it out of an attitude of rebellion. God will not honour it long term, and you will model to the children in your care some attitudes that are the very opposite of those brought by the Spirit. So go to your leaders, share your vision, and ask if that is OK with them. They may well be happy with it without personally wanting to go in that direction, but if they are clearly in opposition, to go ahead would be wrong. Perhaps you should find a church with whose leadership you can agree, and go and work there. That's a hard thing to say, but I do believe it needs saying.

But what of the third corner of the triangle, the family? To this we now turn.

11

Children in Families

I've argued that the context created by God for children to grow into the things of the Spirit is the family, but I've been somewhat ambivalent about which family. You may have spotted a potential problem when you read that bit, and it's to that problem we must now turn our attention. I made the point in the previous chapter that children will really catch fire for the Lord if they are being nurtured not just in their Sunday or weeknight groups, but also within the context of the whole church, and of their human families. As we move to examine the role of the family, we need to answer two main questions.

The first concerns parents who are either ignorant of or antagonistic towards our aims as children's ministry leaders. Put plainly, aren't we likely to run into conflict with children's parents if we as church people start to influence their off-spring, and especially if we influence them in some of the slightly unpredictable ways of the Spirit? For instance, what are little Johnny's mum and dad going to think when he comes home one Sunday morning and tells them he's started to speak in tongues?

This question is of course a complex one, and it will need

to be dealt with under several headings, according to the spiritual state of the parents in question. Some, for example, may be totally outside the life of the church and have no real understanding of what it means to have faith. Their child is simply there due to the evangelistic efforts of a friend. In my leadership of children's ministry I have always put a high value on outreach, and the children have been encouraged in all sorts of ways to pray for and to invite their friends. Occasionally we ran 'Bring-a-Friend' mornings, which the children themselves designed, and with which their parents (and indeed the whole church) co-operated. To a reasonable degree these mornings were successful, and we ended up with a number of children who were there without their parents. Members of the church who lived near them agreed to pick them up and bring them (and used the excuse for the steady building of relationships with their parents), and mostly they settled in well.

But doesn't this create problems? You would certainly think so, but in my experience it simply doesn't. You might expect us to have had angry complaints about brainwashing, indoctrination, turning children funny and so on, but in fact we've never had anything of the sort. While the parents themselves may seem to have no desire for a faith (or think they've already got a totally satisfactory one), they are without exception grateful for the fact that their children are being exposed to spiritual things. Some, I suspect, are actually a bit wistful and envious of their children's growing spirituality, which may well evoke for them happy memories of their own Sunday school and the halcyon days before the church let them down by becoming irrelevant. No doubt this is not true for all parents, but it is likely that the really antagonistic ones wouldn't let their children anywhere near us in the first place. The fact that children are allowed to come at all demonstrates a degree of openness on their parents' part.

You may be ministering, of course, in an area where children's parents have not the first idea where they are at any given time, and would take no interest at all in their spirituality. In that case use the freedom you've got to involve children as much as you can. There will be plenty of other forces out to get them, so you might as well fight for what is right. And then you can make deliberate attempts to build bridges to and relationships with their parents.

This is potentially a very fruitful area of ministry. Back in the 70s some of us were told that to use children to bring parents into the church was a bad thing to do. Now the tide is turning and we're beginning to realise that contacts made through children are important. So don't be afraid of non-Christian parents and what they might say; build friendships with them instead.

A different problem may arise if the parents are Christians but quite honestly find all this charismatic stuff weird and terrifying. Again the secret seems to be relationship. If the parents know the leaders, or the parents of other children in the group, and find them to be fairly normal human beings, they are likely to trust them. If their children do come home with weird ideas every once in a while, an opportunity for witness and explanation is opened up. If the point is reached where parents really do feel that their children are stepping outside the boundaries of Christian orthodoxy, they may choose to withdraw them from your group and even from your church, but this is an extreme case which I personally have never encountered. It is far more common in my experience for parents to move children out of a church because it is too dull, not because it's too lively. And if the fruit of the Spirit is steadily growing in their young lives, their parents ought to be able to notice and be glad.

A third category of parents would contain those who for one reason or another have never been taught about discipling their children, possibly because they have come into a living Christian faith more recently. If their children are older they may have done most of their parenting without the benefit of James Dobson's help,[1] and in their attempts to co-operate with the Spirit now, they are in fact trying to move in a new direction. The more you teach on the Spirit, and the more you seem to require of children, the more threatened and de-skilled they will feel.

The problem with people in this position is that they won't want to talk to you about this. So you do need to go out of your way to keep the communication channels open, and to set up opportunities for airing the issue. You'll need to remind them that we're all living in dysfunctional families, and that you certainly haven't got everything right yourself, but that you have discovered some things that can help. Above all you want to give the message that it's never too late, and that God's redeeming love is always available to those who seek it. Once this relationship and understanding has been established, you can begin to share a few skills with them. Many people would testify to the effect committed prayer has had on youngsters they may have regarded as past redemption. You may feel able to offer to join them in regular prayer for their family.

And finally, what of the culture shock to children whose parents have had a 'Damascus Road' conversion experience, causing everything to change? If the new Christian parents head in the direction of super-spirituality, children can be left bewildered and resentful. They never used to pray at all, but

---

[1] *The New Dare to Discipline* (Kingsway, 1999) by James Dobson is a classic guide to Christian parenting.

now it's happening all over the place: before their breakfast, before they decide whether to go to the park or the swimming pool, and even, horror of horrors, in McDonald's! Christian tapes have ousted Radio One from the stereo, and every Sunday morning now needs to be spent in the presence of those creeps who keep hugging one another and 'sharing'. Who can blame children for a bit of rebellion when this lot suddenly drops on them?

The message to parents here is: Go easy. Children may take time to catch on, and the more dramatic their change in lifestyle, the longer it may take. You'll need to encourage them to win their children over, little by little, and not to be discouraged if they don't seem to be moving at the pace they'd like. They can be encouraged to talk to their children about the whole thing, to be honest about what's happened to them and any mistakes they feel they've made in the past, and they'll need as well to do lots of listening to understand what it feels like from the other side. You can't decide who children will be friends with, but there may be opportunities to encourage them to build relationships with other children from the church, if to do so would seem natural and not another bit of pushing. But in the end it comes back again to the fruit of the Spirit: if God is truly at work in the parents, the children will recognise that fact because they'll become better parents.

The second question I'm wanting to answer in this chapter is a much more positive one: How can parents who are fully in sympathy with what your church's children's ministry is trying to do, and who want to co-operate as much as they can, work with leaders and the church to see their children growing in the Spirit? It may not come completely naturally, so I'd like to change focus and address for a while parents in that position. Let me give you four practical pieces of advice.

1. Take an interest

It is very easy for children's work leaders to feel isolated from parents. If you have, and communicate, the attitudes we've mentioned about regarding them as mere baby-sitters while you worship, you'll be severely undervaluing them (unless of course that is how they regard themselves). So you'll need to take positive steps to show that you care about what they're doing with your children each week.

You can do this, first of all, simply by asking, 'How's it going? How is my little Johnny fitting in? Is he happy?' Add to this some feedback: 'He's really enjoying the series you're doing at the moment on Leviticus. He particularly loved last week's session. Do you know what he said when he got in? And that evening in his prayers he spoke to God in a way that proved he'd really understood about the mildew regulations. He loves the model too – it's right by the side of his bed.' This could include questions too: 'Could you explain again what you were doing the other week about infectious skin diseases? I don't think he quite understood.' In the context of relationship (there's that word again), this kind of conversation can help to mould you together as a team concerned with Johnny's spiritual welfare.

You could ask to visit one Sunday. Some groups will build this in anyway with a parent-helper's rota, but others ought to welcome the interest you'll bring, as long as you go in with the right attitude (we'll talk about this in a moment). If you do visit, don't communicate the feeling that it's a great sacrifice really, and you'd much rather be in church. Do all you can to build up and encourage those who regularly miss out on teaching because they place your children higher on their list of priorities than they do themselves.

You may like to take this even further by inviting your children's ministry leader to your home group, Mothers' Union meeting or whatever to tell you about their vision and what they do week by week. And while you're at it, ask about the pains and frustrations of the job – you'll be surprised how many there are. Talk about how you can support one another in your different areas of ministry, and keep children's work on your prayer list. It's a frontline ministry and it needs all the power and protection it can get.

And leaders too have a responsibility here. It is vitally important that you remain open about what you're doing. If you are seeking to allow the Spirit to move among the children with his supernatural power you may feel the whole thing to be a little risqué, especially if the church as a whole is less than happy about it and you are in a pioneering position. The tendency to get a bit masonic about it, and restrict the details of what you do behind locked doors to the initiates only, must be resisted at all costs.

So how about an occasional meeting between children's work leaders and parents, where you set out clearly your vision for the ministry and invite comments, questions and co-operation? However pioneering you may feel your work to be, most parents will probably be working with a much more traditional view of what they imagine you're doing than is actually the case. At best they may regard you as purveyors of Bible stories, and at worst they may simply be grateful to you for looking after their kids while they get on with their worship and teaching. This needs challenging, their imaginations need stretching, and they may not turn out to be anywhere near as suspicious as you might expect.

When over 15 years ago I was first given a slot at a whole-church prayer meeting simply to explain my vision, as set out in Chapter 3, I was greeted with a standing ovation from the church as a whole. They had little idea as to the revolutionary nature of what I had been doing. They knew their children loved going, but that was about it. Hearing in detail not just about what was going on, but why it was going on, enabled them to buy into and rejoice in the things God was doing among their children. The whole profile of the children's ministry in the church was raised significantly. So keep the lines of communication open, in both directions.

2. Recognise the partnership

Those who are both parents and schoolteachers will understand something of the tension this can cause. At school they may sometimes feel (although of course never be so unprofessional as to say) that some parents who try to help, for example with reading, have no idea what they're trying to do, and cause more problems than they solve. But at home they may hear about how their little Sally has been treated at school and exclaim, 'But they don't know her as I do!' Here lies an issue that can also appear sometimes in the church's ministry to children. Where there is tension between parents and leaders, it can be not because of what each does know, but because of what they don't.

So leaders need to understand that they have Sally for perhaps an hour each week, while her parents have her for a good deal longer than that. However much they think they understand, they simply can't know her as well as her own family do. Parents, on the other hand, need to appreciate that the children's team are doing that job because they have been called and anointed to it by God and recognised by the church as having at least some of the skills required. So while the leaders may not know Sally as well as they do, they may well know a lot more about how to teach and lead children into discipleship. They're not perfect, of course, any more than most parenting is perfect, but they do basically know what they're doing.

Because our family has had to move around quite a lot, our children have had to change schools, and the contrast between the openness and welcome to parents in different schools has been striking. Particularly notable was our move to the People's Republic of South Yorkshire. At the Sheffield school we were allowed into the building, we could sit in on lessons any time we wanted to, we looked on the teachers as our friends, and neither party felt threatened by the other's role in the care of the children. By contrast, we have been given the message elsewhere that we were not welcome any further than the school gates, and that the staff were perfectly competent thank you very much, and would do a much better job without our interference. For children's leaders to foster relationships and co-operation will be a very large plus.

There is the potential here for great co-operation, as long as those on each side of the equation know their own roles, strengths and weaknesses, as well as those of the other side. So it won't simply be a case of handing your offspring over for an hour a week; rather you'll work in partnership at providing what's best. There is also obviously the potential for great conflict as each side guards their boundaries jealously, but to take one's eyes off one's own insecurities and focus instead on the spiritual welfare of the children will help to minimise this. If you do feel uneasy, talk about it. Otherwise the Enemy will do all he can to drive a wedge between you.

3. Learn the skills

If your family life is not backing up the work of the children's ministry and giving children the same experiences, a tension will be set up. So parents need to be heading in the same direction, and learning to minister to their children in the same ways. Reread Chapters 4 to 7, and ask yourself how much of this material is put into practice in your own family prayer times. Are there healings, like the one we mentioned earlier? Is there an expectation that God will speak prophetically through words or pictures as you pray together? In the final chapter I'll be developing the point I made earlier about the fact that adolescence is the great time of trial, when all that children have learned will go through the fire of reality-testing to see if it will pass the ultimate examination: 'Does this work?' If the Spirit is active in supernatural ways in our families, the reality is established. If your children's work involves the use of spiritual gifts, which hopefully I have by now convinced you that it should, you as parents will need to begin to acquire some of the same skills so that they can be integrated into family life.

The same goes for the Bible. I needn't labour the point again here, because I've tried to make it a constant theme throughout this book. But it is a knowledge of the Scriptures which will ensure a correct use of the Spirit's gifts and encourage the growth of his fruit. It isn't enough just to buy some Bible reading notes for your children, any more than just buying them a toothbrush guarantees dental health. They'll need you there beside them to help them do it and sometimes to make them do it.

I said above that it's primarily the leaders who bring a knowledge of the Spirit and the Bible to your children, but that doesn't mean parents are let off the hook entirely. That would be as wrong as telling the leaders that they needn't bother to get to know the children, because the parents do that bit! There needs to be a partnership, but the overlap must be constantly growing.

4. Be worship leaders

In Matthew 21 we read about the children who joined in the
worship of Jesus as he rode triumphantly into Jerusalem. A
great crowd of people were following him, and it is interesting to compare their worship (v. 9) with that of the children
(v. 15). Notice anything? It's the same. Children are great imi-
tators: what they see adults doing, they do. A little girl nurses
her doll, dresses and changes it. How? In the same way she
has seen her mum do it to her baby brother. A car is fitted
with a little plastic stick-on steering wheel for the kids in the
back seat, and they copy the driver's every move. This is one
of the main ways children learn, and in this passage it is the
way they learn worship. Now here's a terrible question to
have to answer: If the children in your church were to imitate
the way their parents worship, what would they do? In fact,
there's no 'if' about it; they will. Parents need to learn how to
lead their children in worship, both at home and in church.

But there is one model that is very helpful for parents,
although it is very commonly neglected. If your church is the
sort that has someone who is called a 'worship leader', or if
you've ever seen worship leaders in action at Spring Harvest
or a similar event, think for a moment about what they do, or,
more particularly, what they don't do. Their job is to facilitate
the worship of the congregation, but this is a highly sacrificial
role. They cannot, for example, get too involved in what is
going on. They can't get spaced out in wonder, love and
praise because they have to have one eye all the time on the
congregation, so that they can meet their needs. But neither
can they just be directors while remaining totally uninvolved,
because as we've said you can't lead from behind. So they'll
say things between songs, which will encourage people or
focus their worship. Sometimes they'll emphasise particular

lines and apply them. And on a more mundane level they'll have practical tasks too, like telling people where to find the next song or paragraph of liturgy, when to sit or stand, and so on. Those who lead worship generally manage to enjoy it and meet God through it, but it is a sacrificial rather than a selfish task. They may feel strongly at times that they'd like to go and receive some prayer ministry, or they may feel moved to dance or wave flags about, but they resist those desires, for the moment at least, since that's not what they're there to do. They are there to serve others.

What's that got to do with children? The fact is that if they are in church with their parents, children, and particularly young children, need their own personal worship leaders, and Mum and Dad are the people to do it. It is sad to look around some churches and see lots of adults in rapt states of worship while their children are busy eating hymnbooks, playing noughts and crosses, or, even worse, simply sitting there bored out of their minds. No one has bothered to lead them anywhere.

My conviction is that parents who come to church with their children have the same role as the worship leader at the front. At times they will be whispering to their youngsters, telling them which page they're on, and, even better, pointing to the words as we go through them. As the leader at the front may occasionally exhort us to 'lift our voices together' as an encouragement in worship, so Mum may whisper to little Billy to 'sing up'. When the leader tells us all to keep a few moments' silence to enjoy God's presence among us, Dad can echo this to Billy, enforcing it if necessary!

You see there is a fallacy around this area: freedom is not necessarily a good thing. If we have the freedom to worship or not, there are times when we'll choose to not, because it requires less effort to sit there in a stupor. But when a leader encourages us, we make the effort and find that it was well worth it, since we've encountered God in a way that just wouldn't have happened unless we'd been told to put some work in. The same is true with children. They won't naturally join in with worship in church, particularly if it is intended for a wider age range than just theirs. But by cutting down their other options and helping them to do the task in hand, parents are actually setting them free to worship – free, that is, from the other things they'd rather do but which would do them less good. Parents do this all the time, for example whenever they make their children eat salad rather than just chips, so why baulk at doing it in worship? That's why I mentioned in an earlier chapter the discipline of children by their parents during worship. We're not being hard on them if we demand that they stay involved, but rather we're setting them free from other distractions in order that they can worship.

But it does need to be understood that this is a sacrificial ministry, and parents need to recognise that they will only have one eye available for God if the other is to be kept on Billy. That's why it's important that at times they worship without him being present (Billy, that is, not God), either because he's out with the children's group or because he's in bed for the evening with a baby-sitter. But to get on with it yourself while leaving him to his own devices will do nothing to help him grow in the Spirit. In fact the opposite may be true: his boredom may lead to disenchantment and more serious long-term consequences.

So, there are some hints for parents about working together with the children's ministry and the church as a whole. 'A cord of three strands is not quickly broken,' says Ecclesiastes 4:12. By tying together these different influences on children, the work of the Spirit in them will be enabled and enhanced. A strong foundation for the future will be built, and that future will be met with an abiding faith in Jesus. For the final chapter we'll take a look into that future and see what might change as our children grow up.

12
Growing Up

So far most of what I've said has been mainly applicable to younger children, and you may perhaps have found this a little frustrating. If your children, or the children you work with, are moving on into adolescence, you may have read so far with a sense of wistfulness and nostalgia for the days when it was as easy as that. But now it's different, and a whole new set of rules seems to apply. Is there anything that can be helpful to those working with older children and teenagers?

At one level the simple answer is 'no'. This is not a book about youth work. Neither can I claim any vast experience with teenagers, although of course like most curates and wives John and I have done our stint with the church youth group. But we did so without much in the way of enthusiasm or flair, and neither of us has ever really considered it our calling. But what we do have is the experience of having steered two sons through adolescence, so perhaps on one level there may be one or two things I can say which will be helpful for those facing or preparing to face the dangers, toils and snares of this particular stage in life.

It is, of course, with the most extreme diffidence that I

169

write this chapter. The earlier version, *And for Your Children,* which I wrote in 1993, was in comparison blissfully easy to write, since at that stage our boys were nowhere near adolescence, so I could be as theoretical as I liked, and hope for the best that things would actually work out in due course as we had planned. But we're now emerging from the other side of this phase (although we have yet to face it with our daughter, which might be very different). I can no longer claim ignorance, and those who know us well will know some of the painful traumas through which we have had to pass. However, the encouraging thing is that there is very little of the theory which we would want to change in the light of experience. If we had our time over again, I think we'd stick pretty much with what we thought and wrote all those years ago from our state of blissful innocence. So the rest of this chapter is pretty close to the original, although perhaps a bit less naïve in places.

The first thing to say is that as parents we can plan ahead. Our lack of direct experience of adolescent children did give us a certain naïve objectivity, but the reflecting we had done about the earlier stages of our children's development could, we felt, be extrapolated a bit further. And of course like everyone else with eyes and ears, we were able to observe some of the things going on around us, and some of the mistakes we saw being made by others. And looking back, that was how we learned quite a bit about what we know about children.

John and I got married rather later than most of our peers, and then waited a further five years before Steve was born. So while we were in the blissful state of freedom, many of our friends were well into babies, toddlers and even fully fledged children. We never studied parenting to any great degree at that stage, but we were often to be heard remarking on the way home from visits, 'When we have kids they won't behave like that!' It was experiences like these which taught us much of what we learned, and we sought to put them into practice when we did start a family. Our friends, had they overheard us, could well have given us knowing looks which said, 'You wait!' We knew nothing; we had no experience of what it was like to cope with a two-year-old's tantrums or any of the other horrors that formed their daily diet. And yet the objectivity we did have enabled us to set out principles that subsequently proved to be successful (in as far as our parenting can be judged to be successful, which mercifully most of my readers will never know!).

First of all, I would want to question the tacit assumption that our children will turn rebellious and nasty when their hormones get going at about 13. There seems to be a resignation and terror in many if not most parents that they are in for several years of hell, which will end up with their children rejecting totally all they have been taught for the first dozen years of their life. I believe that it doesn't need to be like that. Job, in the midst of his pain and suffering, exclaimed, 'What I feared has come upon me; what I dreaded has happened to me' (Job 3:25). Those experienced in the world of counselling would point to this verse as a key one for understanding pain and fear. It's almost as if we will bring trouble onto ourselves if we worry about it too much.

Many parents – including, amazingly, many Christian parents – have bought what I believe to be a lie, and when it does work out as they feared and expected, they shrug their shoulders and say, 'I told you so!' The Bible, which is never afraid to give warnings when difficult times lie ahead, says nothing about the need for adolescence to be a tragedy. Our whole culture has been cursed with this expectation, and the more it does happen, the more we believe the curse. I firmly reject this, and our experience is that though the adolescent years have been taxing, they haven't been totally disastrous. They may be, of course, for some families; nobody is denying that. But we do not need to bow to the inevitability of it. We're not under the control of the teenage years – we have some control over them. Whether or not they prove to be one long tragedy will be affected to a high degree by the way we handle them and what we expect from them.

This ought to be good news for parents approaching this phase, but it also lays a big responsibility on them, and it may lay a great deal of guilt on those who feel they have failed in some way. If it's true, we can't just blame hormones – we could ourselves have helped things to be different. Now my desire is not in any way to load guilt on people, but a true understanding of the situation is a good place to start in the work of redemption, for which, as I've mentioned, there is plenty of grace with God. So what is going on in adolescence, and how can we help it to pass with as little trauma as possible?

First, there are of course physical changes taking place. Hormones do cause temper tantrums, mood swings, sudden fluctuations when our little baby becomes a loutish oaf and vice versa. That is a biochemical fact, and the Spirit's power is not given to bypass this process. And there are psychological changes too, with the growing distance between parents and children, an increasing need to question and test the assumptions they've lived with all their lives, and the traumatic realisation that Dad and Mum are not Superman and Superwoman after all. All this was built into us by our creator God as part of the process of letting go, and it is basically a good and necessary process, extremely painful though it can be at times. The question is: Where is the dividing line between that which God has created good, and that which through sin the Enemy has spoiled? Where can we expect the sanctifying work of the Spirit to make a difference, and where mustn't we expect him to bypass the important but painful work of separation into adulthood?

It's not only family relationships which can be affected by adolescence. Statistics have shown that the teenage years are the stage where the greatest number of people lose their contact with the church and their faith (and, conversely, where the greatest number find faith). Many Christian parents are saddened by their teenagers' rebellion against them, but even more so by their rebellion against God. As we've already seen, traditional Sunday school methods have quite simply failed to hold on to children successfully. When we were confronted in 1991 with the statistics for church decline from 1979 to 1989, we were told that 40 per cent of the 1,000 people who stopped going to church each week of those ten years were under 15, and 87 per cent were under 30. Even in some of the denominations that are experiencing net growth, there is still decline among the child membership. All in all, we have no evidence whatsoever to suggest that the way we've been doing children's ministry in the past has worked. Is there any hope that the greater exposure to the Spirit that this book argues for will make any significant difference? The only answer to that is 'Time will tell', but it is my conviction that the work of the Spirit ought to make adolescence less traumatic, if not totally trauma free.

Let's begin to answer some questions, first of all by asking another one, and then by looking at a case study. The all-important question is: 'What are adolescents searching for?' If we can understand that, we might be able to see how we can help them find it.

The search for stability

So much is changing, in teenagers' bodies, minds and circum-
stances, that they can end up confused and angry. Anything
that can bring stability into this bubbling cauldron of uncer-
tainty will do a tremendous amount of good. They probably
won't be able to articulate their need for it, and they may kick
very hard against it (more on this later), but they desperately
need it. Those whose parents split up during this period, for
example, will speak eloquently of the added pain this caused
at an already difficult time. On the other hand, those whose
home and church life was stable are able to see, even if only
in retrospect, the value it was to them.

When we were in parish ministry a few years ago a little
boy in our congregation was very ill, and spent a long time in
intensive care. It really was unclear whether or not he would
pull through, but eventually he did, and returned home, amid
great rejoicing in the church family. But he was different. He
would go into fits of uncontrollable temper, or sobbing, or all
kinds of other antisocial behaviour. His parents, while grateful
for his recovery, were filled with anxiety about him. They
knew from their experience of counselling that severe traumas
can sometimes allow access to demonic forces, and John was
called in to pray with the boy. While believing in the possibility of such oppression, he found it hard to imagine how someone who had been so soaked in prayer throughout the illness
could have fallen prey to the Enemy in this way, so he phoned
a friend who was both spiritually experienced and a doctor
working with children. Was it common, he asked, for children
to be disturbed in this way? The answer he got contained a
profound message which is equally applicable to adolescence:
if someone begins suddenly to behave differently, it is usually
because they have been treated differently.

And so it was. For weeks little Simon had been the centre of attention: he could eat, or leave, what he felt like and sleep or wake when he felt like it; his crying was immediately treated with sympathy and comfort; there were people around to cater for his every need, instantly, and finally his grateful parents, so relieved to have him safely back, indulged him with all sorts of treats and fed him up to help him regain the weight he'd lost. John did go and pray, but the prayer was not for major deliverance. It was when the parents began to treat their son consistently again, and to re-establish the behaviour boundaries that had previously been enforced, that his tantrums began to subside and he made a full recovery.

When the adolescent tantrums first appear, it is very tempting for parents suddenly to throw all the rules out of the window as if a terminal illness has set in. When a teenager needs stability more than ever, this is a big mistake. So we must try to make sure that we keep up the family standards of behaviour which we've always expected. Our children should, as it were, be able to sing to parents and to churches, as well as to God, 'O Thou who changest not, abide with me' when all around (and within) is change and decay.

The search for independence

Second, adolescence is about the search for independence: becoming a person in one's own right, and not just an extension of one's parents. Painful though this is for both parties, it must happen. The first time they go out on their bikes alone; the first day at secondary school; the first Scout or Guide camp; the final holiday all together as a family; the new motor-bike; even the first time they sit with someone else in church: all these are great traumas for parents, but vitally important for the kids. Parents may be left feeling obsolete and superfluous, and that hurts after they've given the best years of their life to their children. They may resent rather than welcome the growing relationships with other adult role models, such as youth leaders, which it is so important for young people to develop. They may even feel envious of the opportunities young people have nowadays which they simply didn't when they were young, and this envy may lead them into a subconscious limiting of their children's experiences.

Then of course there are the dangers young people encounter. The fear of parents is that once their offspring are out of their control, all manner of disasters too terrible to articulate will befall them. And of course, it has to be said, they might. That's why it's so frightening. The art is to know when to allow and when to forbid any attempt at independence, and to know why.

This independence is not just about physical separation; it is about intellectual distancing too. Values we've taught need to be examined and often rejected, at least for a while. This may show itself in dress style and behaviour patterns. There is almost the desire to shock for its own sake, but also a burning need to fit in with the peer group. John spent most of the late 60s trying to sneak out of the door with his mum's fur coat on inside-out (he couldn't afford a real Afghan) before his dad caught him and told him he wasn't going out looking like that. Wise parents will realise that the battle has nothing to do with clothing and everything to do with independence. Parents who are secure in their relationship with their teenagers can save themselves considerable pain by a deliberate choice of which battles to fight and which to choose to lose. If every little thing becomes a major issue, with bad feelings around 24 hours a day, life can get very uncomfortable. So why not choose the important battles to fight, and let them have a funny hairstyle if they want?

The same issues apply on a spiritual level. I've already said that many children are unlikely to find a spiritual home in the same church or tradition as their parents, but the anxiety caused by their first trip to the New church down the road can be every bit as great as any of the above forays, and the perceived dangers just as great. Thus we react with fear and possibly anger. To cultivate a trust that they are in God's hands, and to rejoice that they are healthy enough to begin to venture out, is difficult indeed. But the more we try to stop them, the harder they'll try to go. Why? Because God has built into them the need to go, and rightly so.

The kind of discipling we do with young children can affect deeply this quest for spiritual independence. If we teach them, directly or by implication, that our church is the only real one, the struggle to find a spiritual home later will be that much harder. But if we build in an understanding that there are in all the different tribes those who are God's people, and even that they may well one day want to move to a different tribe, the move if it comes will be much smoother. Some churches seem more interested in building an empire than in building the kingdom. Children will pick this up, and it'll provide one more thing for them to kick against later. But if we set bigger boundaries within which they can explore and find their place, the whole exercise will be that much less painful.

The search for experience

The teenage years form a time when new experiences await at every turn. Part of the nature of adolescence is a desire to explore them to the full. Sex and drugs and rock 'n' roll are out there to be discovered, and whether it is their first Benson and Hedges or their first charismatic service, there is a thrill in the new – a thrill enhanced if the new is also slightly naughty.

Again, this can be a threatening time for parents, who are very aware of the dangers but totally oblivious to the fact that they did exactly the same things themselves and are still here to tell the tale. (Or, alternatively, it may be that they remember only too well their own experiences, and want to protect the next generation from the mistakes they made!) This is often where the crunch comes with church. Bible stories may have been fine up to this point, but lots more is needed if they are to stick around.

The search for reality

Along with this comes a testing out of all they once held dear. Particularly this holds true spiritually, where all the things they've been brought up to believe and value are interrogated with one big question: 'Does this work?' If they've been brought up with Christian values and Bible stories, they'll want to know, and to prove by experience, that the whole deal passes this test. And this, as I've already said, is where the church has fallen down with the hardest bump. The things they learned in Sunday school, but which were never applied, are simply irrelevant. The experiences of people in the Bible whom they read about without ever experiencing the same things themselves are just so many fairy tales.

I've explained before my conviction that knowledge and experience must go in partnership, because in the teenage years knowledge is almost equated to experience. A teenager who has only heard from the Bible about healing or speaking in tongues (and even they are sadly few) will stand less of a chance of surviving adolescence spiritually intact than one who has healed or spoken in tongues. Where children's work leaders have taught, parents have backed up the teaching, the church has made space for him or her to minister, and personal experience is still present – that's reality. There are no double standards or hypocrisy or hollowness (all of which youngsters can sniff out a mile away), and nothing to suggest that this needs questioning. It works!

The search for purpose

The teenage years are those during which a new, personal identity must be found. Particularly within the church family, there is a need to make a mark and find a niche. It is an idealistic time, with high hopes and high principles abounding. Our world and its prince, threatened by the potential power of this idealism if God were ever to get his hands on it, have managed to divert it onto safer issues like rain forests and baby seals, but if our children's ministry has taught children to dream dreams for God instead, there is tremendous power waiting to be unleashed.

Some children feel quite early a calling from God on their lives. This must of course be tested and refined. Our Paul decided strongly at one stage of his life that he wanted to be a milkman; it took some time before we twigged that this calling appeared at a phase when we were constantly sending him back to bed in the morning because he was getting up too early! The thought of being on the road by 5 a.m. legally was captivating for him! But if the church and families don't take this growing need for a calling and purpose seriously, and help their teenagers to see that people's standing before God is an even more important issue than dolphins getting trapped in tins of tuna, teenagers will be beset by spiritual self-doubt and will try to find fulfilment elsewhere. The good can indeed be the enemy of the best.

The search for security

But there is one thing above all which teenagers require during these difficult years: security. One youth worker told me that the thing which really touches streetwise teenagers is to see people who are committed to them. In all sorts of ways they need to kick against the boundaries they will perceive to have been hedging them in until now, but they need to know that there are some boundaries that will not move. They need to be sure of their parents' love, and the acceptance of the church family. It's almost as if some of them will go out of their way to test it: 'You say you love me? Well love me after *this*!' Rules are disobeyed; rooms are left untidy (no change there from childhood); surliness, rudeness and arguments follow one after the other: '*Now* love me!' comes the challenge. But if we don't, their whole world crashes in. It's a bit like when you come downstairs in the dark and think you've reached the ground, only to find you've miscounted. Suddenly there's nothing there to put your foot on, and it's all you can do to stop yourself from tumbling headlong. 'Prove you love me, and prove your stupid rules still apply': that's the challenge.

If these are some of the things teenagers are searching for during adolescence, can the Spirit help them and parents and churches to provide them? Let's look at a case study to end this chapter, and let's use one particular family in whom the Spirit lived more fully than any other. It'll be an interesting study, because it'll help us to see how things should be, since the Spirit lived in one member of the family totally and completely, but it'll also show us reality, because the other members, like us, are not perfect. The incident in question is recorded for us in Luke's Gospel, chapter 2.

Jesus is twelve – not a bad age for an adolescent. He's with his family, doing what they always do (v. 42). There's the stability. The adolescents in many of our families would be lying with the covers pulled up over their heads, saying, 'Mum, do I have to go to the Temple this year?' But Jesus went.

Then there's the independence (vv. 43–44). He's in the crowd, they think, but he'll be OK. He's big enough to be trusted without wearing his reins any longer. For a whole day he's on his own, and isn't even missed. The problem is that he's not in the crowd at all; he's out looking for experience (v. 46). Maybe he's already felt the call of his Father on his life to be a rabbi and a teacher, so he wants to see how it feels to be with some.

He's also searching for reality. There's a discussion going on. He's been rooted and grounded in the Scriptures, but he wants to know more. It would be fascinating to know what he was talking to the teachers about, but sadly we're not told. But clearly he wants to know, and he's wanted to know for three solid days.

His parents arrive and he gets a telling off – not totally unjustified, we may feel. But his answer shows that he's found purpose (v. 49). He's now got a higher purpose in life; his Father, rather than his parents, is now calling the shots. But note finally the security he finds (v. 51) as he remains obedient to his earthly parents and returns to normal family life, as far as we know, for the next 18 years. The outcome? 'Jesus grew in wisdom and stature, and in favour with God and men' (v. 52).

We've looked at this story from Jesus' point of view, but what about his parents'? Look at the emotions involved, and see if they ring any bells for you. The anxiety, first of all, as they discover he's missing, and the terrified searching, which lasts for three days. The relief at finding him, which shows itself in anger. The exasperated cry of, 'Why have you treated us like this?', and the total incomprehension of his answer to them. All these are experiences that every parent either has known or will know.

So what can we learn, both from the perfection of Jesus and the all-too-familiar reactions of Mary and Joseph? How can we see the work of the Spirit making a difference, and how can we hope to survive the teenage years more or less intact?

Note first of all the politeness of Jesus, and his obedience. He doesn't throw a wobbly when his parents tell him off; he doesn't shout at them or argue with them. Rather he obeys them. The fruit of the Spirit, which has been growing in him for twelve years, is manifested in his even temper and his desire to explain rather than argue, even when his parents don't have a clue what he's on about. There is explanation rather than resentment, and communication instead of withdrawal and sulking. This speaks well of the foundations laid in his heart by his parents and the Spirit working together. Our teenagers may get angry with us, and vice versa, but none of us needs respond in the ways Paul calls 'the acts of the sinful nature' in Galatians 5:19 if we have all grown the fruit of the Spirit, which he goes on to list (vv. 22–23).

Another important principle appears in verse 49, with Jesus' words 'Didn't you know . . . ?'. 'This shouldn't have taken you by surprise,' he's saying. Neither should our children's adolescence take us by surprise. With a bit of imagination we can predict the likely issues that will arise, and we can prepare for them. We don't believe it to be inevitable that one of our boys will announce to us one day that he is moving in with his girlfriend, but neither will we be completely taken by surprise if he does. We've got our answer ready. This proactive style of parenting means that we won't need to be reactive. In other words we won't respond out of shock or

anger, and say things we'll later regret. All sorts of likely
issues have already been faced in our imagination, and we
feel as prepared as we can be for them. It's not that we've
never been shocked or angry or hurt – we haven't got that
much imagination – but I don't feel that we've gone careering
through the teenage years tossed about by totally unforeseen
waves of fortune. For the sake of the boys' security we have
needed to retain a degree of control, and forewarned is indeed
forearmed. If you're reading this chapter before the great and
terrible day of the twelfth birthday, you can do things now to
prepare. It will save lots of wasted rage later.

It's not just parents who can be proactive. Our children as
they approach adolescence are approaching a time of great
turbulence. It needn't be nasty, and we can tell them that as
well as believing it ourselves, but it will be strange. We found
it very helpful to begin working with Steve through a book
called *Preparing for Adolescence*,[1] which helps young
teenagers to get ready for some of the things they'll experience over the next few years. Even if it doesn't help the actual
process, it certainly can take some of the shock away, and it
opened up all sorts of subjects for discussion. The talks themselves were helpful, but even more so was the lesson that we
can talk about things like this.

Trust in God's faithfulness is another quality the Spirit
brings to us. Parents may need this a lot more than their children do, and it won't make us totally immune from anxiety,
but ultimately all things work together for good if we're
God's people. Of course we'll worry, but we can model to our
children a simple trust that will be a great stabilising influence
on them during the tumultuous years they go through.

---

[1] James Dobson, *Preparing for Adolescence* (Kingsway, 1982).

Note as well that discipline never breaks down in this story. At the start and at the end Jesus is subject to his parents. The boundaries may have been strained a little, but they haven't moved. Jesus' parents have made it possible for him to obey both his earthly (v. 48) and his heavenly (v. 49) fathers. So often we set up false dichotomies, even as Christian parents. If the worst bit of rebellion your children come up with is that they want to change to the Pentecostal church, you're fortunate indeed. Don't make a big issue of it; thank God that they still want to go somewhere. Thousands don't!

The big issue here is serving God. Jesus' heart is set on that, even if it isn't in quite the way his parents (or his home synagogue) were expecting. It is sad when churches stifle attempts by teenagers to do something significant for God because it doesn't fit the style or ethos of the church. And it is wonderful when the leadership can see the desire there and make space for it. It may need refining, but then so do most of our ideas, if we're honest. Bill Hybels runs the largest church in America, the famous Willow Creek Community Church near Chicago. It began when he formed a partnership with a musician called Dave Holmbo and started to run Bible studies attached to music rehearsals. From a youth group of 25, he now leads a church with a Sunday attendance of 15,000 people. Yet many times along the way things could have been threatened by the church authorities.[2] So it may be that among the crazy ideas your youth groups come up with there is a real winner. How sad to miss out on it, and how rejecting for those behind it. It's as if Mary got Jesus home and said to him, 'That's the last time I let you out of my sight!' If only our churches could learn to treasure the things our youngsters are

---

[2] You can read the Willow Creek story in Martin Robinson, *A World Apart* (Monarch, 1992).

trying to teach us. In my experience it is those churches that have opened their life consciously to the wind of the Spirit which are more happy to take risks, and which are more likely to expect to hear him speaking in unexpected ways, even sometimes through teenagers!

This hasn't been the last word on adolescence, but I have attempted to show how the Spirit can help. The writer of Proverbs (whoever he was!) wrote these words: 'Train a child in the way he should go, and when he is old he will not turn from it' (Proverbs 22:6). The principle here is that what we do with children will affect how they turn out as adults. It's no good waiting; you need to get started right away.

I very much hope that this book has given you some practical hints about how this training up might be achieved in partnership with the Holy Spirit, whom the Father gives so that we might be holy and Christ-like. There's no money-back guarantee; after all, it is people we're dealing with, and they're all different and special. But they're all special to God too, and I wouldn't want them to miss out on anything he might have for them. The promise of the Spirit is for us who believe and for our children. Let's do all we can to help them receive that most precious gift.

Children's Ministry Teaching Programme

- Do you want to see children develop a personal relationship with Jesus?

- Do you want teaching sessions that are fun, biblical, evangelical and interactive?

- Would you like children to enjoy age-appropriate activities as they learn about God?

If you've said YES to any of these questions, you need the Children's Ministry Teaching Programme.

The Children's Ministry Teaching Programme provides four leader's guides covering ages from under 3 to 13+; KidZone activity books for children aged 5-7, 7-9 and 9-11; MiniKidz and KidZone craft books for children aged 3-5 and 5-9, a magazine for those over 11; a CD of music and stories; and FamilyZone with song words, ideas for all-age worship and parents' letters.

**For more information visit our web site
www.childrensministry.co.uk**

100 Worship Activities for Children

by Chris Leach

This practical resource gives ideas for activities and games that illustrate the true meaning of worship, to help lead children into a deeper relationship with God.

Many are also suitable for all-age services, designed to bring new life and exuberance to your church's worship time.

The ideas are listed under seasons of the church year, with full theme and Scripture indexes.

Reclaiming a Generation

Children – today's church, tomorrow's leaders

by Ishmael

From the author's Introduction:

'I have written this book because I believe it is time to re-evaluate our many traditions, and as we do so, I pray that it will make us more understanding of what the Bible says is expected of our children.

Before you make up your mind to agree or disagree, just look outside your window and ask yourself honestly how the thousands of lost little ones around you will ever get to know Jesus, or get to love the church, if we just stay as we are for the next two thousand years.'